# Evolutionism
and
# CREATIONISM

by Ben Sonder

**FRANKLIN WATTS**
A Division of Grolier Publishing
New York / London / Hong Kong / Sydney
Danbury, Connecticut

Photographs ©: AP/Wide World Photos: 96 (Christopher Berkey), 5 (Ben Garver), 45; Archive Photos: 56 (Popperfoto), 31 (New York Times Co.), 28, 34, 48; Art Resource, NY: 41 (The Pierpont Morgan Library); Corbis-Bettmann: 29, 66, 80, 86 (UPI), 33; ENP Images: 74; Gamma-Liaison, Inc.: 8 (Hulton Getty); North Wind Picture Archives: 24, 60; Photo Researchers: 39 (A. Barrington Brown), 10 (Miguel Castro), 76 (E. R. Degginger), 43 (David A. Hardy/SPL), 16 (Marine Biological Laboratory/Mark Marten), 15 (Mary Evans Picture Library/Science Source), 72 (John Reader/SPL), 13 (Science Source), 19 (David Gifford/SPL), 64 (Michael Tweedie).

Visit Franklin Watts on the Internet at:
http://publishing.grolier.com

Library of Congress Cataloguing-in-Publication Data

Sonder, Ben. 1954-
    Evolutionism and creationism / by Ben Sonder.
       p. cm.
    Includes bibliographical references and index.
    Summary: Examines both sides of the creationism versus evolution debate from the mid-nineteenth century to the present.
    ISBN 0-531-11416-3
    1. Evolution (Biology)–Juvenile literature. 2. Creationism–Juvenile literature. [1. Evolution. 2. Creationism.] I. Title.
QH367.1.S65   1999
231.7'652'0973–dc21                                    98-53650
                                                       CIP
                                                       AC

# Contents

# CHAPTER 1

# A Battle over Science Education

Merrimack, New Hampshire, is the kind of town you don't read much about in the national news. Most people who live in this small community of 22,000 never intended to end up in the limelight. They concern themselves with what goes on just outside their front door. New Hampshire has traditionally frowned upon strong, centralized government and has given towns like Merrimack a high degree of local control. Maybe that's why most people in 1994 were so ill prepared when a conflict arose that threatened to tear apart this peaceful community. It was a battle that set neighbor against neighbor and won the attention of the national media.[1]

The conflict began when Reverend Paul Norwalt, a local Baptist minister, complained that the Merrimack school system was biased against religion. Why, he wanted to know, did schools teach evolution, which was only a theory, without also teaching the theory of creation? He took his complaint to the school board, which considered it seriously.

By "evolution," the minister meant the scientific theory that all living things develop over millions of years from previous life forms. Included in this theory is the subtheory that humans are descended from apelike ancestors. By

*The Reverend Paul Norwalt speaks at a Merrimack, New Hampshire, school-board meeting in support of teaching creationism.*

"creation," the minister meant the belief that life on Earth was created just as it appears today by God, in only six days and just a few thousand years ago, as recounted in the Book of Genesis in the Bible. According to Genesis, humans did not descend from apelike species. God created them in the form they exist in today.

When the school board of Merrimack finally decided that it would replace its science textbooks with books that included discussions of both evolution and creation, the battle exploded. Charles Mower, a school-board member who opposed the change, sputtered, "This used to be a progressive town 50 miles north of Boston. Now we're just a gooberville in Arkansas!" Mower singled out Arkansas because about a decade earlier the state had passed several laws requiring that the creation theory be taught in any school that also taught evolution. Virginia Twardowsky, a board member who had supported the change, was infuriated. "I've been sitting here listening to all these evolutionists speak and speak, and they get up and tell us evolution is an absolute fact," she said. "I'm more convinced than ever before that creation science has got to be taught in the schools!"

Twardowsky was voicing a feeling shared by a significant faction of Merrimack parents. The evolution experts who were called in to speak about the issue had only made some people who believed in creation feel belittled. The scientists had an obvious bias against those who thought the history of life on Earth could be entirely explained by the Genesis chapter of the Bible. And to many parents, the scientists also seemed contemptuous and haughty.

Meanwhile, those who believed in evolution education were getting increasingly offended. Things heated up when the creation education supporters invited Duane Gish, co-founder of the California-based Institute for Creation Research, to Merrimack. The Institute for Creation Research had been established to gather and promote scientific evidence that the Genesis version of life on Earth is true. When Gish was offered the high school cafeteria as a place to make his speech in favor of equal time for creationism, parents who wanted their children taught only evolution began fuming. "Don't try and teach my children that creationism is a science," said one parent. "It's not. We want to prepare our students for the 21st century."

On the surface the fight between Merrimack's factions may have looked simple enough. But beneath the two positions lurked pressure cookers of resentment and fear. In a way, the battle between evolutionists and creationists was a battle between two American cultures with radically different world views. For many creationists, the battle symbolized the struggle in this country between religion and godlessness. For many evolutionists, it represented the choice between scientific progress and ignorance. And in the minds of members of each side, the enemy had become a frightening stereotype. The creationists tended to lump those who believed in evolution education with those who favored liberal causes, such as condom distribution in the schools, gay rights, and ample social welfare benefits. The evolutionists saw the creationists as religious fanatics, "right-wingers," or hopelessly misinformed "hicks." As each faction fought for its way, newspapers throughout the nation turned their attention to the little town of Merrimack. Some said the battle raging there was for nothing less than the American mind and the American soul.

## DARWIN'S NEW IDEAS

How many of the parents who fought this battle knew that it had been developing long before it exploded in Merrimack? In fact, the conflict between evolutionists and creationists dates back to the first half of the nineteenth century, when some major tensions between religion and science were established.

In 1831, a young English student of religion named Charles Robert Darwin graduated from Cambridge University. Through the influence of an older friend who was a naturalist, Darwin found a position on an English ship called the H.M.S. *Beagle.* The ship was traveling around the world, and Darwin would serve as its naturalist. During the voyage he would study and catalog all the animals and plants he encountered.

At the time Darwin began his voyage on the *Beagle,* most European scholars believed that extinct life forms no longer existed on Earth because they had been destroyed by sudden catastrophes, such as earthquakes and floods. These scientists thought that the last great catastrophe had been Noah's Flood, as described in Genesis. The Flood had wiped out all the animals that Noah had not taken onto the ark. The animals that were taken onto the ark

*When Charles Darwin embarked on his voyage as ship's naturalist on the* HMS Beagle, *he had no idea that he would change the face of inquiry into the origins and processes of life on Earth.*

had survived, and their descendants lived today. The animals that stayed behind had been drowned and buried under mud. Eventually, they became the fossils that were discovered centuries later.

According to this theory, dinosaurs, apes, humans, dogs, carrots, and mushrooms—in fact, all life forms that ever lived—existed at the same time, in the same form, and from the very beginning of creation. The theory didn't allow for any hereditary links between the species, since all were created by God in an unchanging form. All that it allowed for was the elimination of some life forms by catastrophe, which was supposed to explain why animals such as the dinosaurs no longer exist. This theory about the appearance and disappearance of Earth's life forms is sometimes called "catastrophe theory" or "catastrophism."

Respected scientists believed it during Darwin's time, and it influenced the scientific study of the Earth's crust as well as the study of biology. The theory produced very little conflict between scientific thinkers and proponents of the ideas about life on Earth set forth in Genesis.

Darwin spent his entire voyage on the *Beagle* collecting samples of animals, plants, and fossils. As his supply grew, he began to doubt seriously the catastrophe theory. There was, at the time, a noted geologist who also disagreed with it. His name was Charles Lyell, and in 1830 he had attacked the catastrophe theory in a work called *Principles of Geology*. In its place, he proposed the theory that the Earth was always changing slowly and in small increments—not just by catastrophe. And Darwin thought that Lyell might be right. Perhaps ancient life forms had not been wiped out by sudden catastrophes. Perhaps their descendants had developed over many generations into new forms of life.

During his voyage, Darwin noticed that the fossils of some extinct species bore a close resemblance to species currently living in the same area. This led him to the supposition that the current species might have descended from an older species that had died out. The idea of gradual yet radical changes in species over time conflicted with the story of creation in Genesis, but it had already been suggested as a possibility by thinkers as far back as the ancient Greeks. In fact, almost fifty years before Darwin's voyages, a French naturalist named Jean-Baptiste Lamarck had done extensive research in an attempt to develop this theory of gradual descent. Lamarck had cataloged similarities between different species, such as the cat, the leopard, and the tiger, and proposed that they might all have descended from a common ancestor.

One of the *Beagle*'s stops was the Galapagos Islands, off the coast of Ecuador. There, Darwin found even more evidence for his theory. The islands were very close to each other, but each seemed to have different species of the same type of animal. For example, there were 14 species of finch distributed among the islands. Each had a distinctive body form and a different set of behaviors. Darwin later speculated that the ancestor of all these birds might have been a single species of finch. The original birds had come from the mainland and then separated into groups that ended up on different islands. Perhaps, he thought, over many generations the characteristics of the finches on each island had changed, producing the 14 species that he observed.

If this was so, what had made the animals change? By taking a close look at his data on the finches, Darwin was able to determine that each finch species was suited perfectly to its environment. The major differences among the species were the shape and size of their beaks. On islands where insects were plentiful, the finches had thin, sharp beaks suitable for picking them out of the dirt. But on

*Darwin's study of the differences between finch populations on the various islands of the Galapagos archipelago played a major part in his formulation of the theory of natural selection.*

islands where seeds were more readily available, the finches had strong, blunt beaks for cracking hard seeds and nuts. On another island there was a species of finch that could use its beak like a tool, grasping a thorn from a cactus that grew on the island to dig out grubs from holes in trees.

By the time Darwin got back to England, he had developed theories about how these species of finch had developed their different characteristics. His theory was based in part on an essay by a British economist named Thomas Robert Malthus, who maintained that populations of humans always grow faster than the available food supply. Malthus thought that population sizes were automatically adjusted to the food supply by bouts of famine and disease. These events killed off some people, constantly reducing the human population to match the amount of food available.

Darwin applied the same theory to animals and plants and combined it with known principles of plant and animal breeding. He eventually came up with a concept known as *natural selection*. Other naturalists had already observed that communities of animals compete for a limited food supply; only those which survived could produce the next generation. Those that died off left no descendants, and their unique characteristics disappeared from the species. These individuals were the least well adapted to their environment. Those that survived to reproduce successfully were the most well adapted. In other words, they and their characteristics had been "selected" to survive by nature.

The finches on the Galapagos Islands served as a good example of Darwin's new theory. On an island with a food source of hard nuts and seeds, those finches with the bluntest, strongest beaks had survived and passed these characteristics on to their offspring. Finches with long, narrow beaks would have died there, but would have survived on islands with abundant insect populations.

It would take a few generations before scientists could offer any proof for some aspects of Darwin's theories. But Darwin's ideas that animals who were best adapted to their environment had the best chance of survival made sense. Several questions remained, however: What produced the variable physical characteristics that led to these different survival rates? Also, how were well-adapted physical characteristics passed down to descendants? After all, people had seen parents produce descendants that did not exactly resemble them.

In the mid-nineteenth century, Austrian monk and botanist Gregor Mendel conducted research on genetics and demonstrated some of the rules of inheritance, but as his research was conducted in a monastery, his works went largely unnoticed. Subsequent discoveries also showed that populations within all species produce mutations— chance variations that lead to rare, abnormal physical characteristics. Mutations introduce new traits into a population. If these mutated traits increase an individual's chances for survival, and therefore reproduction, the occurrence of the traits increases as well. Finally, these become the dominant traits, and a new species arises.

In 1856, Darwin announced his theory of natural selection, prompted by a young naturalist named Alfred Russell Wallace, who had independently arrived at the same ideas. Darwin expanded his own theory in a book called *On the Origin of Species*, which was published in 1859. The book changed the study of biology forever, but it also permeated nearly every domain of scientific thought. Never again would religious beliefs and the scientific method co-exist as comfortably as they had before. If one species of animal could slowly develop into another resulting from chance events affecting the available food supply and chance adaptations to it, then the idea that God created each creature exactly as it is was cast in doubt. In fact, Darwin himself stated that his main goal in writing *On the Origin of Species* was "to overthrow

# THE ORIGIN OF SPECIES

## BY MEANS OF NATURAL SELECTION,

OR THE

### PRESERVATION OF FAVOURED RACES IN THE STRUGGLE FOR LIFE.

By CHARLES DARWIN, M.A.,

FELLOW OF THE ROYAL, GEOLOGICAL, LINNÆAN, ETC., SOCIETIES;
AUTHOR OF 'JOURNAL OF RESEARCHES DURING H. M. S. BEAGLE'S VOYAGE
ROUND THE WORLD.'

LONDON:

JOHN MURRAY, ALBEMARLE STREET.

1859.

*Publication of Darwin's* On the Origin of Species *in 1859 was the spark that started the controversy between creationists and evolutionists that continues to this day.*

the dogma of separate creations." However, at the beginning, Darwin made some attempts to remain true to a godly view of the universe. In his book he made statements that seemed to assume that someone or some force had created the very first living being on Earth from which the other forms had descended and evolved. He did not say that this creator was God, but his language and his vagueness left room for those who believed in God to speculate that this was so.[2]

In 1871, Darwin published a second book, *The Descent of Man*, which left little doubt about his opinions of biblical views of creation. In *Descent*, Darwin claimed that humans descended from a four-legged, hairy creature with a tail and pointed ears. The creature, he said, would be classed in the same group as the ancestor of today's monkeys. This ancient ancestor was, in turn, probably the descendant of a more primitive creature—a marsupial. And the marsupial's lineage could probably be traced all the way back to "some fish-like animal." Such ideas were practically an out-and-out contradiction of the story of Adam and Eve in Genesis.[3] Even so, religious thinkers of the time were not ready to dismiss Darwin's ideas out of hand. Some of these thinkers tried to come up with methods of reconciling Darwin's theories with the story of creation as it is presented in the Bible.

## EARLY REACTIONS TO DARWIN

In the few decades after *On the Origin of Species* was published, Darwin found partial support among scientists who never totally gave up their creationist views. One of his most enthusiastic supporters in the United States was Asa Gray,[4] a deeply religious botanist. Gray accepted much of Darwin's theory but hoped that Darwin would begin to see evolution as guided by some divine power. Eventually, Darwin disappointed him.

*This caricature of Darwin from an 1874 London magazine illustrates public opinion of his ideas on evolution and natural selection.*

Others wrote tracts against Darwin but accepted the idea of variation of species over long periods of time. At Harvard, Swiss-American scientist Louis Agassiz[5] upheld the idea that the species were created specially by God. But he also refused to interpret Genesis literally. He thought that the human race had come from many origins rather than from Adam and Eve and that creation had not lasted six days but millions of years. During this time, he said, many catastrophes and creations had depopulated and then repopulated the Earth.

In general, the early opponents of Darwin were much less extreme than many are today. They believed that fossils had accumulated from living things that had died over a long time period, not just after Noah's Flood. They also granted that the Earth was much older than a few thousand years. And many assumed that the story in Genesis

*Louis Agassiz (1807–1873), a world-renowned naturalist and devout Christian, supported many aspects of evolutionary theory, but he opposed the idea that species evolved into different forms over time.*

was a parable and not the literal truth. Still, a great many suggested that not only natural selection, but God, had had a hand in the development of the species. They believed in a form of divinely guided evolution. And when it came to the origins of humans, they insisted on this idea. Few wanted to think that the human species had come about accidentally, as changes in the environment led to gradual changes in earlier life forms.

Ministers and other clergy of Darwin's time were uncomfortable with his theories but, in most cases, failed to establish complicated arguments against them. Before the mid-1870s,[6] most of them merely labeled Darwin "unscientific" without going into too much detail. As proof, they cited disagreements that had been voiced by experts such as Louis Agassiz. Starting in the mid-1870s, some of the clergy started publishing more involved arguments against evolution. In general, they tried to prove that no one who believed in the Scriptures could support Darwin with a clear conscience. They went to great lengths to prove the ungodliness of the notion of natural selection. However, practically none of these writers insisted that the Earth was only 6,000 years old or that the fossils had all been created by the Flood. It was becoming obvious that, despite objections, Darwin had changed thinking about the origins and development of life on Earth for nearly everyone.

## THE DEBATE INTENSIFIES

Tensions between evolutionists and creationists may have begun gradually, but Darwin's theory was like a cultural time bomb waiting to explode. Naturally, Darwin's theories had their greatest impact in the world of science. Until the time in which he lived, the scientific method had relied heavily on the ideas of sixteenth-century philosopher Francis Bacon. Bacon had revolutionized science by insisting on the gathering of large amounts of precise data. He believed that scientific concepts were born when ideas could be inferred from data. Ideas were formulated by comparing what was observed in individual things with the characteristics of the larger category to which they belonged. Bacon relied heavily upon inductive reasoning, which is reasoning from the particular to the general. Instead of forming theories and then looking for evidence to support them, he preferred to collect facts about the world and then formulate theories. These theories remained unchanged until there were enough facts gathered to contradict them. That's why few scientists who believed in Bacon's methods ended up challenging assumptions such as the truth of the Old Testament. No data were collected to prove that it was either right or wrong.

In Darwin's time, scientists became more interested in deductive reasoning, which is reasoning from the general to the particular. In deductive reasoning, a person formulates a hypothesis early on, then looks for evidence to prove or disprove it. During Darwin's time, many thinkers developed a new tendency toward material, rather than spiritual, explanations of the world. By material explanations, they meant explanations that were based on observable facts and measurable data instead of supernatural notions. These thinkers felt that spiritual, or religious, hypotheses could not be proved or disproved by observable data but that material hypotheses could. Darwin's theory of evolution was one major material explanation of the development of life on Earth. He had abandoned biblical explanations of life on Earth because they could not be proved right or wrong by science.

One thing that bothered some nineteenth-century thinkers about Darwin was his refusal to clearly divide animals from humans. According to most conventional interpretations of the Bible, humans are the pinnacle of creation. They have been put on Earth as the natural masters of all living things. They have souls, whereas animals do

*This illustration depicts many evolutionists' ideas of how humans evolved from a more primitive ancestor. Homo erectus is shown at center right.*

not. When Darwin removed the boundary between humans and animals by suggesting that humans are descended from an apelike ancestor, some people thought he was lowering the human species. They called evolution an insult to humankind and a denial of God's gift to humans. Darwin's ideas wreaked havoc with the traditional ordering of life on Earth, a concept that many had thought could not be challenged. In some cases, such rethinking made animals seem more worthy than they had been thought to be. In some other cases, the rethinking made people feel insulted.

There were even more serious criticisms of the theory of natural selection in the decades after its publication. Philosophers and other intellectuals began applying the ideas of natural selection to other areas of inquiry, and in some cases, the results were very disturbing. As recounted previously, natural selection depends upon the notion that only those animals who are most fit—or best adapted to their environment—survive to reproduce. As interpreted by some thinkers, this theory came close to supporting the idea that "might makes right."

For example, some, known as Social Darwinists, applied the theory of survival of the fittest to human social situations. To understand how, imagine, for example, that some Indians in the Amazon rain forest are being forced out of their habitat by powerful industrialists who want to use the resources for manufacturing. There could be a moral reason for opposing such an action: The Indians have a right to their homes and shouldn't be subjected to force. There is also a practical argument: Destroying habitats in the rain forest is not proving to be beneficial to the world's ecology. But someone could try to use the theory of natural selection to justify driving the Indians out. They could claim that the industrialists were selected by nature because of their characteristics to profit from the environment. With their superior strength they can drive the Indians out, and that's all there is to it. The weaker, or supposedly less-adapted Indians, will die off; the supposedly fitter industrialists will survive. The situation, some would say, is merely natural selection at work.

With varying degrees of logical sense, Darwin's notion of survival of the fittest was applied to political situations again and again. Some used it as an excuse for subjugating people. Others pointed to this possibility as proof of the dangers of Darwinism. They cast Darwin's theories as lacking moral purpose or compassion. They accused him of validating an existence that is unguided and meaningless. They said that, according to him, it is not the good or the just who are rewarded, but the strongest. Since he saw no master or divine plan for the development of life on Earth, it was as if Earth's history were a series of senseless accidents. Conditions in the environment changed by chance, and then new mutations arose that happened to be better adapted to them. The lucky few who inherited these mutated traits became the new winners.

20

# CHAPTER 2

# Modernism and the Scopes Trial

Darwin's theories spread at a time in history when many other changes were taking place. Taken together, these changes led to a point of view called modernism. Originally, modernism was a term used near the beginning of the twentieth century to describe an attempt by intellectuals and members of the clergy to revise Christian thought so that it would be more in line with the scientific thought of the second half of the nineteenth century. Modernist thinkers reinterpreted the Bible as parable or allegory rather than as literal truth. They also pointed out discrepancies, such as the fact that the first chapter of Genesis describes God as creating Adam and Eve together whereas the second chapter says that Adam was formed from dust and Eve from Adam's rib.[1]

These intellectual endeavors weakened the authority of the Church and challenged many time-honored traditions. At the same time, new modes of transportation and communication were changing everyday life. Cities enlarged and brought people who never would have met into contact with each other. Class divisions weakened. The media brought new information to everyone's ears and eyes.

In the twentieth century, modernist thought helped change philosophy and the arts. As an example of this, consider one major facet of twentieth-century modernist philosophy, *existentialism.* Existentialism hypothesizes a world without any particular fixed meaning in which each individual has the responsibility for creating meaning as he or she sees fit. Such an attitude promotes *relativism.* Relativism is the idea that different ideas are true in different contexts. Relativism maintains that behavior considered worthy in one culture may be considered immoral or worthless in another and that neither culture is absolutely right. For example, a good headhunter might be revered by a rain forest tribe but would be arrested in the United States. The same headhunter might interpret hallucinations on the part of a member of his tribe as possession by spirits. But an American would be more likely to interpret the same experience as a symptom of mental illness.

Relativism suggests that there are no absolute truths, only truths that work at a particular time and in a particular place. At its best, relativism promotes an open mind and unbiased judgments. But people who attack relativism, many of whom are anti-evolutionists, say that it leads to immorality. They reason that if there are not strict, unchanging rules about what is right and what is wrong, people will be able to justify the most heinous behavior. Enemies of relativism claim that only a strict adherence to God's principles can offer a plan for right living.

## FUNDAMENTALS AND EVOLUTION

The ideas of modernism made great headway in the early twentieth century. Using science and deductive reasoning as their weapons, modernist thinkers began an attack on certain aspects of traditional religious thinking. Their efforts would eventually lead to a backlash that helped popularize a conservative Protestant movement in the United States that had begun near the end of the nineteenth century. This movement, called Fundamentalism, promoted the idea that all Christians should subscribe to the following fundamental, or basic, beliefs.[2]

1. The Bible is the spoken truth of God to man. It is not allegory or parable and should not be subject to literary interpretation.
2. Jesus Christ is more than a great teacher or prophet. He is divine and is the result of a virgin birth.
3. Christ was sacrificed on the cross as atonement for all our sins. He is the personal savior of each individual and the only way to salvation.

Fundamentalism's roots lie in the Evangelical Protestant movements of Great Britain and North America that began several hundred years ago. Evangelicalism, which comes from a Greek word in the New Testament meaning "good news," stresses the personal relationship of each individual to Jesus Christ. It calls for strict morals, a plainspoken code of religious practice, and the supreme authority of the Bible. From the eighteenth century on, there were several waves of Evangelicalism among Protestant believers in the United States. All of them stressed preaching and outreach to those who were not yet converted. But by the end of the nineteenth century, Evangelicalism in some cases also became a reaction to modernism and the newer, looser interpretations of the Bible, as well as to Darwinism.[3]

In 1909, a twelve-volume work called *The Fundamentals*, written by fervent Evangelists with very conservative religious views, was published in the United States and abroad. Bible institutes, such as the Los Angeles Bible Institute and the Moody Bible Institute in Chicago, began teaching the doctrines expressed in the collection. From the beginning, many Fundamentalists saw themselves as enemies of those scientists who refused to accept super-

*The rise of modernism in the late-nineteenth and early-twentieth century sparked several waves of Evangelical outreach movements. Camp meetings, such as depicted in this illustration of a revival in Duck Creek, Ohio, brought the teachings of religious Fundamentalism to thousands of rural and working-class people.*

natural explanations for some of the world's phenomena.[4] They also took the position that only those who followed Fundamentalist beliefs and practices would be saved from Hell. That meant that Jews and Catholics as well as Protestants who did not take the Bible literally would be damned. This motivated the Fundamentalists to try to save these souls by changing their minds, or converting them, and bringing them into the Fundamentalist fold.

It is not easy to characterize the Fundamentalist movement as a whole, or to separate it from the larger group of Christians known as Evangelicals of which it is a part. However, from the start, and to some degree today, Fundamentalists were more likely to be from the rural and small-town South and Midwest than from the big American cities. They tended to be members of the lower and middle classes, such as farmers, clerical workers, or small-business owners. And compared with non-Fundamentalists, they had less formal education.[5] However, even those without much formal education were often highly educated in the principles of their own faith.

From the beginning of the Fundamentalist movement, Darwinism was singled out as one of the biggest threats to correct Christian thinking, but the truth is that he never got to the point of affirming that there was no "First Mover." Darwin never found an explanation for the origin of the first living thing or for things on Earth from which all the others supposedly descended. He never answered questions such as: "What caused the first living thing to exist?" and "What created the universe itself?" The fact that he didn't provide answers to these questions means that one can be a Darwinian without being an atheist. Someone may not believe in a literal interpretation of the Bible, but can still believe in divine influence on the Earth's history.

Even today, only a tiny number of evolutionists are also atheists.[6] Most of these believe that all natural processes can be explained scientifically and that the origin of Earth and life on it can be accounted for only in physical and chemical terms. If asked how living things first came to exist, they would be likely to describe a chance chemical reaction between hydrocarbon molecules that created the first living matter, and they will maintain that this occurred about 15 billion years ago, without the influence of a "higher power." Such people have become known as nontheistic evolutionists. However, the majority of people who believe in evolution also believe that there is a God. They think that God created the universe as well as the materials needed to make life appear within it. Some of these people also believe that God's plan is ultimately the basis of natural selection. They have come to be known as theistic evolutionists.

There are different kinds of creationism as well. In a very thorough book on the subject of creationism, science historian Ronald L. Numbers outlined the three main creationist points of view.[7] All of them are ways of interpreting the story set forth in Genesis. But some of them try to reconcile this story with Darwin's theories.

Of the three creationist points of view, the one called *flood geology* or *creation science* is the most radical contradiction of Darwin's theories. It maintains that there was probably no life on Earth until about 4,000 or 8,000 B.C. Then, during a six-day period, God created every life form, including the first humans, Adam and Eve. According to this view, all the fossils were formed around 3000 B.C. and consist of animals left behind by Noah during the Flood. This point of view allows for no gradual changes in species and for few interrelationships among species. It denies that any fossil can be older than about 4,000 years. It especially denies the descent of humans from an apelike ancestor.

According to the *gap,* or *ruin and restoration,* creationists, life and matter were created millions instead of thousands of years ago. They assume that they were created by God. Then multiple catastrophes occurred over a long time period, and the remains of life forms that died in these catastrophes were left behind as fossils. God also created new living things during this long period.

This idea allows for the emergence of different life forms at different periods in Earth's history. It is more in line with current scientific thought about geology. Modern geologists and paleontologists believe that the Earth is billions of years old and that the fossil record proves that life has existed on Earth for hundreds of millions of years. But the gap theorists also believe that after one particularly bad catastrophe that wiped out most or all living things, God restored life on Earth. This restoration was supposed to have occurred around 4000 B.C., as described in Genesis. God accomplished this restoration in six days, during which he also created the first humans, Adam and Eve. The theory denies the descent of humans from an apelike creature.

26

The *day-age* point of view is the one that comes closest to the ideas of Darwin. It is mostly a reinterpretation of the six "days" of Genesis as periods of thousands, or perhaps millions, of years. On the first "day," meaning in the first long period, matter was created by God. On the third "day," life was created, and on the sixth "day," humans were created. This point of view allows for Noah's Flood but suggests that it might have been local, rather than worldwide. Fossils were probably produced in between the time when life was created and humans were created by God.

There are many variations of these three positions, and some come even closer to the evolutionist point of view. For example, there are "old-Earth creationists," who acknowledge that the Earth is much older than is indicated in Genesis and who are willing to accept the fossil record as partly true. There are others who accept all of Darwin's theories but whose outlook is that Earth's events have always been guided by the will of God and that the Bible is also an important tool to an understanding of this process.

When all points of view are taken into account, the strict division between evolutionists and creationists begins to blur. Are people who believe in God and evolution evolutionists who believe in creation; or are they creationists who believe in evolution? The boundaries between the two world views have been unclear since the start. It was only at the beginning of the twentieth century that they began to organize into the opposing factions at the forefront of today's major battles.

## THE SCOPES SCANDAL

By the early twentieth century, it had become more evident that the evolution controversy in America was actually a struggle between modernist and traditional viewpoints. Tensions between the two philosophies came to a head in

*High school teacher John T. Scopes allowed himself to be used as the test case for the court case that brought the evolutionist-creationist argument to the forefront of American society.*

the summer of 1925 in a town that seemed just as unlikely as Merrimack, New Hampshire, to become the center of national media attention. The town was Dayton, Tennessee, and a young schoolteacher, John T. Scopes, had been arrested there for teaching evolution to public school students. By teaching evolution, Scopes had willingly violated the Butler Act, which had outlawed evolution in Tennessee public schools on the grounds that it contradicted the Bible.

The Scopes trial was one of the first trials to capture the attention of the entire country. One-hundred-fifty reporters from all over the world came to Dayton to cover it. Radio station WGN in Chicago, which broadcast news about the trial daily, became the very first station ever to provide a national hookup. But the real story was that the Scopes trial had been staged. The American Civil Liberties Union (ACLU) had been advertising statewide for a volunteer who was willing to break the Tennessee law and offer himself as a test case. Scopes, who had been chosen to serve as the ACLU's volunteer by the city fathers, in hopes of putting Dayton on the map, actually knew little about evolution. The American Civil Liberties Union expected him to lose the case in Tennessee. Then they planned to bring the case before the United States Supreme Court and the eyes of the entire nation.

Another group who thought they had much to gain from the attention that would be lavished on the trial were the Fundamentalists. They formed a coalition made up of deeply religious Protestant groups from all over the country who wanted creationism taught in the schools. One of the spokespeople of their movement was William Jennings Bryan, a man whose varied political career reveals some

*William Jennings Bryan makes his opening statement in support of the creationist viewpoint at the 1925 Scopes trial.*

unusual links between the creationist position and other traditional American values.

In many ways, Bryan would be considered a liberal today. He had run for president three times on the Democratic ticket as a defender of Populism, a midwestern farmers' and workers' movement that sought to raise farm prices, nationalize railroads, and institute a graduated income tax. It was, above all, a people's movement, as its name suggests. It championed the rights of the common man over the interests of big business, and it attracted many lower middle-class and lower-class voters.

Bryan also supported other controversial causes, such as the growing women's suffrage movement. He campaigned for Woodrow Wilson at the 1912 Democratic Convention. When Wilson won, Bryan served as secretary of state. Throughout Bryan's career, he often tried to promote peaceful diplomacy, even advocating that America remain neutral after the outbreak of World War I.

Although Bryan could be called a liberal today, it isn't easy to find a liberal who sympathizes with the creationist cause. However, Bryan's sympathy for the common folk, an attitude that could also be called liberal, made him identify with rural people of the Midwest. He was highly suspicious of sophisticated city journalists and the intellectual establishment in the Northeast. In those days, rural life still tended to be guided by the principles of the Bible. People living in small towns encountered few lifestyles that differed from their own. The complicated ideas of modernism seemed far away to many of them. Many rural people identified modernism, as well as evolution, with America's big-city publishers and journalists as well as the Ivy League intellectuals in the universities of the Northeast. Just as it does today, the New York City publishing industry had a strong influence on public opinion, but many small-towners could not identify with its values.

Another aspect of Bryan's liberalism that put him at odds with Darwin was his reaction to some social Darwinists who claimed that World War I had been a great test of natural selection. Bryan had gone so far as to suggest that all American imperialism was a result of the theory of survival of the fittest—the belief that might makes right. For him, World War I, in which Christian killed Christian, was disgusting. So Bryan's crusade against evolution had a deep moral basis. His brand of liberalism was a vision of a world saved by the Christian values of charity and doing right.

Bryan's opponent—chosen by Scopes—was Clarence Darrow, a Chicago lawyer. Like Bryan, Darrow was a crusader for social causes and a defender of the underprivileged. He was, however, more associated with that world of urban liberals and educated intellectuals resented by Bryan's supporters. He was an agnostic, someone who

*Scopes (center) poses here with his defense team, lead attorney Clarence Darrow (right) and Dudley Field Malone.*

believes that there is no proof of God's existence but does not deny the possibility. He was also known for his defense of controversial clients. These ranged from the labor organizer Eugene V. Debs to two college students named Nathan Leopold and Richard Loeb, who were tried for and convicted of the murder of a fellow schoolboy.

The case of Leopold and Loeb, which had occurred the year before, must have infuriated most strict believers in the Bible. During the trial it was hinted that the two students had killed the boy as a kind of experiment based on the ideas of nineteenth-century philosopher Frederick Nietzsche. Nietzsche's theories of power and creativity suggested that certain individuals had the right to forge their own personal value system and had much in common with the ideas of modernism and relativism. In one of Nietzsche's most famous works, he boldly asserts, "God is dead." By this he meant that traditional values had lost their meaning for most people. Nietzsche claimed that the strong person can create his own value system and that only the weak, who have a "slave" mentality, need to believe in the ready-made values of religion. In the eyes of many who believed literally in the unquestioned authority of the Bible, Leopold and Loeb's insane behavior was an example of what could happen when such an authority was ignored. Darrow's main objective during the trial was to prevent the students from being executed, since Darrow was an opponent of capital punishment. In the end, Darrow managed to reduce the sentence to life imprisonment.

From the beginning, it was fairly obvious to most Americans that the "monkey trial," as it was called, was a contest between small-town and urban America, between religion and science, and between old-fashioned values and modernism. But by this point in American history, there were many powerful forces on the side of the urban modernists. Members of the national press, most notably the witty, biting journalist H. L. Mencken, descended on the small town like vultures. Mencken was a master of mockery. He helped turn the Scopes trial into a sideshow. In referring to the area of the country where the trial was taking place, he coined the term "Bible Belt," which suggested that the region was dominated by Americans who had no other source of learning or information than the Bible.

For newspaper readers in the big cities, the press painted the people of Dayton as hayseeds and naive fools. They poked fun at Bryan and said that he was a spokesman for the past, not the new century that was in progress. Not very well known at the time was the fact that the nation's first popular science news provider, Science Service, was also involved in the trial.[8] Science Service had been founded in 1921 as a publisher of articles on scientific topics. Its main goal was "to promote science as the basis for social and economic progress." Because the service was interest-

*The Scopes trial brought a carnival atmosphere to the small town of Dayton, Tennessee, as each side of the evolution-creation debate tried to get its point across.*

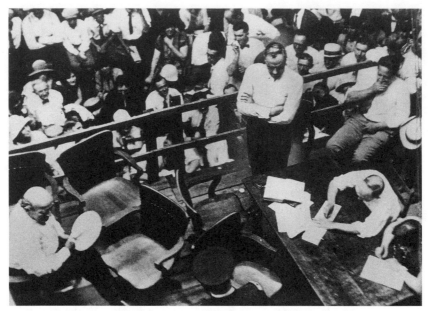

*Clarence Darrow questions William Jennings Bryan on the witness stand.*

ed in portraying scientists as modern truth-seekers, it willingly provided witnesses to the trial who favored evolution. It also provided financial aid to pay Darrow. Science Service sent out bulletins giving news of the trial's progress as well.

Science Service also wired telegrams to world-renowned scientists asking them to give expert testimony, and sixteen of them offered to speak up in support of evolution. Bryan, who was defending the creationist cause, also began looking for scientists who would testify for the state and present evidence to support his point of view.[9] However, he didn't turn up very many who were willing to stick their neck out for his cause. He asked George McCready Price, one of the most resourceful defenders of the creationist point of view, to come back from a teaching post in England to testify at the trial, but Price refused. As a matter of fact, although Price strongly opposed the teaching of evolution in public schools because he thought it ignored the rights of those who believed in Genesis, he also opposed the teaching of Genesis, because it defied the American rule of separation of church and state.[10] Other noted creationists also disappointed Bryan. Alfred Watterson McCann, who had written an acidic condemnation of evolution called *God—or Gorilla* (1922), surprised Bryan by turning on him and accusing him of trying to keep people from thinking for themselves.[11]

The climax of the trial and Bryan's biggest humiliation came when he was cross-examined as an authority on the Bible by Darrow. Darrow asked Bryan to explain such perplexing biblical problems as where Cain's wife came from, since the only other humans on earth before she was mentioned were Adam, Eve, and Abel. Darrow also wanted Bryan to give a precise definition of how the serpent walked before God made it crawl. Although Bryan knew his Bible well, he could not hold up to the precise criticisms of it. When it came to answering whether the six days of creation were really six 24-hour days or six long ages, his answers seemed contradictory to many. When he finally left the witness stand, he had reason to feel defeated and embarrassed.

Nevertheless, Scopes was convicted. This is mainly because the question was whether or not he had broken a state law, not whether or not evolution was true. He was fined $100 and the ACLU got ready to take the case to a higher court. But a technicality concerning how the fine was applied reversed the decision and the matter stopped there. Bryan left the courtroom still convinced that the crusade against evolution would continue. But he was exhausted by what had happened and died suddenly about a week later.

After the Scopes trial, the antievolution movement seemed to wane. An antievolution bill was passed in Arkansas near the end of the 1920s,[12] but as a rule most similar new bills in all other states failed. Meanwhile, those that were already on the books tended to remain. Depending upon the school district, teachers either ignored them when they came to the part of their course that dealt with evolution or taught biology from the creationist point of view. But for the time being, as far as the media was concerned, the issue was dead.

By the 1930s, the evolution-creation dispute no longer seemed like a national issue. The supporters of creationism still promoted and taught it in Christian colleges and private Christian schools, from the Church pulpit, or in religious pamphlets. Scientists in most of the well-known universities continued to discuss, teach, and study the theory of evolution. The discipline of biology became more and more a discussion of the principles of evolution and genetics. Still, mainstream Americans stopped hearing about the subject, not only because the media had lost interest but because school textbook publishers had undergone a change.[13] The turmoil of the Scopes trial had scared some textbook publishers into silence. Before 1925, many textbooks had discussed evolution in detail. Now, if it was discussed at all, it was couched in neutral terms like "development." The publishers may have been working in big-city environments where people tended to favor establishment science over literal readings of the Bible; they themselves may or may not have believed in the theory of evolution; yet when it came to making a living, they wanted to satisfy as many customers as they could.

# CHAPTER 3

# The Birth of Creation Science

In the years that followed the Scopes trial, it may have seemed to the average American as if the "monkey wars" were over. But behind the scenes, each side was marshaling its forces. The trial had made it clear to both evolutionists and creationists that the only way to win others to their point of view was to offer evidence, or at least something that produced a feeling of certainty. Darwinian evolutionists believed their evidence would come from further scientific research and inquiry into the theory of evolution. Some creationists felt that the word of the Bible was enough. Other members of the creationist movement had become convinced that their movement needed scientific underpinnings.

Fresh theories and discoveries during the first few decades of the twentieth century provided a firm groundwork for evolutionary thinking. For a while, advances in genetics had begun to overshadow the preoccupation with evolution. Mendel's basic principles of heredity, which had been published in 1866 but were ignored for more than three decades, were now being rediscovered and developed. Mendel had hypothesized the existence of hereditary units, passed down in a variety of pairings to offspring from their parents. Twentieth-century scientists built on

Mendel's basic notion of gene pairs. They created models for the development of species over time as new genes are produced by random mutations, then passed on to succeeding generations. Ideas about genetic mutation would eventually play a key role in explaining the changes that lead to evolution.

At first, no one could find any relationship between genetic developments and changes in the environment. Without an environmental factor, the idea of natural selection was meaningless. However, when researchers began looking at the distribution of genes in large populations, a link to the environment was discovered and the theory of natural selection was revised.

In 1937, geneticist and zoologist Theodosius Dobzhansky published a book called *Genetics and the Origin of Species*. In it he described experiments with fruit flies that showed how large populations adapt genetically to changes in the environment. According to his data, mutations occur in very low percentages of the total population, at a fairly constant rate over generations. Those that prove favorable to survival are passed on and become more and more prevalent. When the environment changes, a whole new set of characteristics becomes favorable and certain new kinds of mutations are favored by it.

Dobzhansky's studies brought the idea of natural selection back to the forefront of discussions about evolution. They suggested that gradual changes in species were not merely random but were a direct result of environmental pressures. This strengthened Darwin's arguments to a high degree. Some scientists began to propose that the entire study of biology depended upon an acceptance of his theory of evolution.

Evolutionists were given even more powerful support for their point of view in 1953. In that year, James Watson and Francis Crick discovered the structure of DNA, the chemical map of heredity. DNA, they found consisted of

*Scientists Thomas Watson and Francis Crick discovered the structure of DNA, the double helix, which helped explain much about genetics and heredity.*

series of genes, each made up of paired units. Each pairing dictated a trait or set of traits exhibited by each living thing. Mutations now could be explained as random changes in the chemical makeup of genes. This made it possible to trace evolutionary development on the molecular level.

## THE NEW CATASTROPHISM

Meanwhile, the creationists were looking for arguments that were just as compelling. Their newest strategies lay in attacking some scientific assumptions connected to evolution. As early as 1902, George McCready Price, who was a member of a strict Christian sect known as the Seventh-day Adventist Church, had written what he claimed to be the first Fundamentalist science book, called *Outlines of Modern Christianity and Modern Science.* Price thought that the entire argument of evolution depended upon geology. If he could prove that modern assumptions about geology wrong, then evolutionary theory would collapse.[1]

Much of Price's argument focused on something called the geological, or stratigraphical, column. The geological column is a reference to a hypothetical core through the Earth's surface that is composed of a series of vertical layers, or strata. Preserved in each rock stratum, according to most scientists, are fossils of the organisms that lived at the time the stratum was deposited. Those that died earlier are buried in the lower strata. Those that died more recently are buried nearer the surface. In reality, the column is not so precise or simple. There are still many discrepancies that have not been fully explained. In places on the Earth, layers that once were assumed to be older are on top of those assumed to be younger.

Such apparent discrepancies are what Price had been looking for. What would happen, he wondered, if the explanation of geology could be based on events in the Bible? If so, then the most important geological event of all time was a worldwide catastrophe called the Flood. Perhaps the Flood had been caused by a sudden shift of the Earth's axis that had spewed up massive amounts of underground water. First, smaller animals had been swept away, and they had settled into the mud according to their specific gravity, or, roughly, their weight. Fish had died and floated to the water's surface. Larger animals and humans ran to hilltops and mountain tops to escape the flood, but finally it reached them. They drowned and were covered with sediment in the years that followed. In other words,

*This thirteenth-century manuscript illumination depicts scenes from the Flood, which many contemporary creationists cite as the cause of fossils and geological formations used as evidence for evolution.*

the fossils in the strata were not the remains of organisms that lived at different times. All had perished together in the Great Flood.[2]

Price set down nearly all his ideas in a book called *The New Geology*, which came out in 1923 and sold more than 15,000 copies. His theories came to be known as the New Catastrophism because they maintained that most changes on Earth had been caused by only one catastrophe—Noah's Great Flood—rather than by the multiple catastrophes theorized by nineteenth-century geologists.

Throughout the 1920s and 1930s Price kept up his attack on the evolutionist establishment. In 1938, he and some other Seventh-day Adventists formed the Deluge Geology Society. There were strict requirements for membership. All had to believe that the Earth was created in six days and that the Flood was the cause of most of the Earth's geological changes.[3] That left out many creationists, such as those who believed in the day-age theory—the idea that each of Genesis's days were actually long periods of time. The society also banned creationists who believed in the gap theory, which states that there were many catastrophes that produced fossil remains before God created the universe, Adam, and Eve in six days.

Despite their emphasis on geology, Price and his supporters did not garner as much attention as they had hoped. Many other important evangelical scientists had already formed another society called the American Scientific Affiliation (ASA). Its purpose was to discuss science and religion from a Christian point of view. The affiliation came to tolerate many liberal views about creationism. In fact, most of its discussions centered on the fine points of evolutionary theory, often with a goal of revising it rather than getting rid of it all together.[4] Slowly but surely it looked as if the creationist position was really softening. It even looked as if most creationists might end up one day calling themselves theistic evolutionists.

# Sputnik and the
# New Biology Curriculum

In 1957, something happened that would lead to changes on both sides of the evolutionist-creationist controversy. The United States was in the midst of the Cold War—a long period of hostility and tension with the world's other superpower, the Soviet Union. Ever since the United States had dropped nuclear bombs on Japan near the end of World War II, the world's population had trembled at the idea of another global conflict. On October 4, the Soviets astonished U.S. scientists by sending into space the very first artificial satellite. Until that moment few had known that Soviet scientific research and technological know-how had become so advanced.

The Soviet satellite was called *Sputnik 1*. It weighed less than 40 pounds and it was only about 23 inches in diameter. But its impact on U.S. culture made it seem as if it were a million times that size. For the rest of 1957, *Sputnik*, which looked like a metal ball with a TV antenna and

*The launch of the Soviet satellite Sputnik in 1957 sparked renewed concern about the scientific readiness and capabilities of U.S. students and served as a major setback to the creationist movement.*

transmitted a radio signal, was probably mentioned more times by U.S. children than Mickey Mouse or Donald Duck. The *Weekly Reader*, a national newspaper for school-children, did a feature on it. Cartoonists throughout the nation gave it a personality. In the school yard, children mimicked it, twirling in circles with their arms held out like antennae and chanting, "beep, beep."

In the halls of Congress, there was a darker mood about the new toy from the USSR now orbiting the heavens. The fact that the world's greatest Communist power had been the first to conquer space panicked many Americans. What would happen as more and more space vehicles produced by our archenemy surrounded Earth? Would they ever be capable of carrying missiles? Would the Soviets one day set up space stations and planetary colonies that were hostile to the United States?

Most lawmakers were convinced that every effort had to be made to catch up with the USSR's impressive scientific and technological accomplishments. Nearly all agreed that the United States had fallen behind because American science education was deficient. In reaction, Congress voted millions of dollars toward new programs for research and education. Some funds went to an organization called the Biological Sciences Curriculum Study (BSCS). The purpose of the BSCS was to develop a whole new series of biology textbooks for the nation's schools. They were to be written by professional biologists and would feature evolution as the backbone of all biology study.

When the books were finally available in 1963, almost half of all the American high schools began using them. They were markedly different from the "don't ask, don't tell" biology books that had been used since the Scopes trial. The older books tended to avoid the evolution-creation dispute and teach Darwin's ideas in a softened form, if at all. The new books had a hardline evolutionist point of view.

The BSCS textbooks created tensions in some communities that have continued to escalate to the present day. These tensions erupted in 1965 when a biology teacher in Little Rock, Arkansas, sued the state for its antievolution law because it made teaching part of a BSCS textbook illegal. The law was overturned and reinstated several times. But in 1968 the U.S. Supreme Court, the highest authority in the land, finally threw it out permanently on the grounds that it violated the First Amendment. They said that it imposed a restriction on teaching that amounted to state support for religion. By 1970, every other state antievolution law had gone the same way. It seemed as if creationists had nowhere to turn. Neither the accepted textbooks nor the laws of the nation supported their views.

An earlier blow to the creationist cause had come in a more indirect way. In 1963, a woman named Madalyn Murray, who identified herself as an atheist, sued her

*In 1963, Madalyn Murray, a self-described atheist, sued the Baltimore school system for holding public prayer services in her child's school. She took her case all the way to the Supreme Court and won.*

local school system for holding public prayer and Bible reading in her child's public school. The Supreme Court finally ruled that the practice had to stop because it violated the laws ensuring separation of church and state. Fundamentalists, many of whom were also creationists, were livid with rage. Murray was an enthusiastic supporter of the study of evolution. She was also very outspoken about her disdain for Christianity. At one point she went so far as to publicly say, "For this—the scheme of salvation—you give up a rich, full life; you permit the religious to effectively kill science, to constrict women, to foster war, to control you in every aspect of your being. This scheme of salvation, and no minister or priest has ever said me nay in regard to it, this is Christianity in its essence—and it is nuts."[5]

## A CREATIONIST BACKLASH

The fact that Murray had been able to plead her case successfully in the nation's highest court confirmed every Fundamentalist's fear about mainstream America's "pact with the Devil." The new ruling banning school prayer was, however, neutral about religion. It strove to protect people's private right to practice it as they saw fit without interference from the public sphere. So soon after the ruling, some creationists tried to use it to force textbook publishers to make it clear that evolution was a theory only. Their point was that the insistence on evolution was oppressive to their religious practices. In a few local instances, the pressure worked and curricula were revised, but public-sponsored school prayer was banned, at least officially, nationwide, and many schools continued to teach evolution as an accepted theory.

During this low period for the creationists, it seemed clearer than ever that they had to concentrate on another sector of society: the powerful scientific associations whose endorsements made certain ideas legitimate. On every side it seemed as if the tides had turned against them. This did not, however, stop them from further organizing. Some of those who felt equipped to fight evolution on scientific grounds looked to Price and the New Catastrophism for guidance. But at this point, there was nothing very "new" about it. Those who still supported all the principles of *The New Geology* were few and far between.

In 1957 a well-educated Bible teacher, John C. Whitcomb Jr., and an engineer, Henry M. Morris, teamed up to write a watershed book for the creationist movement. It was called *The Genesis Flood* and was published in 1961. Although the book was heavily influenced by the ideas of Price, it strove for a fresh take on some of the principal controversies. Whitcomb and Morris explained the order of the geological column by claiming that sea animals had died first during the Flood and been quickly buried by mud.[6] The rest of the animals were sorted out by currents of water, which sift out and gather together particles of similar sizes and shapes. Whitcomb and Morris also claimed that humans and dinosaurs had once lived at the same time. As evidence, they talked about discoveries in the Paluxy River bed near Glen Rose, Texas. A geologist there said he had found giant human footprints next to those of dinosaurs and had even supplied them with pictures. Although his discovery had not been confirmed by others and was refuted by many scientists, Whitcomb and Morris decided to include mention of it. By the third edition of the book, however, they had decided to delete the passage.[7] But Morris and others kept mentioning the claim in other books.

According to *The Genesis Flood*, God created the universe and gave Earth all of its life forms in six days. All of the fossils that exist today had to be the remains of creatures that died after the fall of Adam, because before that

*Creation scientists claim that Adam and Eve's fall from paradise is the driving force behind the concept of entropy, by which scientists explain the phenomenon of increasing disorder in a given system.*

time, there was no death in the world. After the fall of Adam, there was a period where death and decay became possible.[8] The authors relate this decay to entropy, a concept that is borrowed from eighteenth-century English physicist Sir Isaac Newton's second law of dynamics, which explains that once disorder is introduced into a working system, that system will continue to become increasingly disordered unless there is energy input. They claimed that entropy is one of the chaotic results of Adam's fall.

The arguments of *The Genesis Flood* rely partly on anomalies in the geological column. One of these is the geological phenomenon of *overthrusting*. According to most geologists, overthrusting occurs when pressures within the Earth act on a portion of strata, pushing it upwards. Eventually it overturns. Since it is now upside down, the order of its strata is reversed. Price and other creationists claimed that overthrusting was not an adequate argument for the reversal of the strata. Price himself pointed out an area of several thousand square miles in Alberta, Canada, and Montana where the geological strata were out of order.[9] Such a large area, he claimed, was too big to have been reversed by overthrusting. He said there were not enough of the telltale edge markings for overthrusting to have taken place.

According to Whitcomb and Morris, life on Earth between creation and the Flood was protected by a great canopy of vapor that produced a greenhouse effect worldwide.[10] They said it gave all of Earth the same mild climate and was the source of the excess water that appeared during the Great Flood. The writers also cited this hypothetical canopy as the reason why they opposed current methods of dating fossils using carbon 14, a radioactive isotope of the element carbon. Like other radioactive substances, it is unstable and decays over time. The time a radioactive element takes to lose half of its radioactive activity is its half-life. By measuring the amount of carbon 14 left in a fossil and comparing it with the amount of carbon also present, scientists can roughly determine its age.

To counter radiocarbon-dating evidence that supports evolution, Whitcomb and Morris maintained that the vapor canopy during the time of Eden had also shielded the earth from cosmic radiation.[11] They said this kept radiocarbon from forming in the atmosphere and reduced the ratio of radiocarbon to carbon. Consequently, the fossils of animals who lived at this time would have had less carbon 14 in their bodies to start with and were therefore really much younger than radiocarbon-dating methods said they are.

The publication of *The Genesis Flood* was nearly ignored by the scientific and educational establishment. Within the creationist movement itself, it met with scathing criticism. Members of the ASA attacked it as a form of pseudoscience. Despite these criticisms, the book went through twenty-nine printings and eventually sold more than 200,000 copies.[12] Creationists still read it today.

Within a few years after its publication, the reaction to *The Genesis Flood* had caused a schism among scientists in the creationist movement. Many strict creationist writers and scientists who supported the book became convinced that other Christian scientists were not listening to them. They were bitterly disappointed with the middle-of-the-road views of most members of the ASA, and it wasn't as if they had anywhere to turn in the scientific community. None of the established scientific journals were willing to publish their writings.[13] From the point of view of most strict creationists, evolution had become a kind of religion before which even Christians were expected to kneel. And the government funded evolution research yearly with large grants. Barely a single dollar went to strict creationists, who claimed they also wanted to do research and bring their ideas into the mainstream.[14]

In reaction to this situation, two creationists, Walter E. Lammerts and William J. Tinkle, invited Morris and others to break away from the ASA and other science associations to form a group that became known as the Creation Research Society.[15] Its major purpose was to keep up discussion and research into the Flood and to prevent young Christian students from turning to evolution. In 1963 the society became a formal one. Of its first ten founding members, some had doctorates in biology, one a Ph.D. in biochemistry, and another a master's degree in biology. The society produced a credo that was worded as follows[16]:

1. The Bible is the written Word of God, and because it is inspired throughout, all its assertions are historically and scientifically true in the original autographs. To the students of nature this means that the account of origins in Genesis is the factual presentation of simple historical truths.

2. All basic types of living things, including man, were made by direct creative acts of God during the Creation Week described in Genesis. Whatever biological changes have occurred since Creation Week have accomplished only changes within the original created kinds.

3. The great flood described in Genesis, commonly referred to as the Noachian Flood, was an historic event, worldwide in its extent and effect.

4. We are an organization of Christian men and women of science who accept Jesus Christ as our Lord and Savior. The account of the special creation of Adam and Eve as one man and one woman and their subsequent fall into sin is the basis for our belief in the necessity of a Savior for all mankind. Therefore, salvation can come only through accepting Jesus Christ as our Savior.

It wasn't long before similar creationist organizations began forming. In 1970, a group of CRS members split away from the parent organism to form the Creation Science Research Center (CSRC) of San Diego. That same year the Christian Heritage College started a creationist research division, which eventually became a separate organization known as the Institute for Creation Research (ICR). In 1981 the ICR began offering a program in graduate studies, which won the approval of the California

Office of Education. However, controversy about the ICR never died down, and in 1989, the state tried to withdraw the approval rating. The ICR eventually won its battle for state approval. As research, teaching, and outreach activities grew, it became the leading creationist society.

Meanwhile the Creation Research Society continued in its efforts to get creationism recognized as a legitimate science. As early as 1964, the society began publishing its own journal, the *Creation Research Society Quarterly*. Over the years its membership expanded into the thousands, but voting members were restricted to those with postgraduate degrees in science. Eventually, the society founded a research laboratory in Arizona: the Van Andel Creation Research Center (VACRC). Its purpose was to encourage a variety of research to back up the basic hypothesis that the story of Genesis was the truest account of the origins of human life.

It seemed to many that the creationist movement was geared for a vital comeback. But first a lot of work had to be done. Creationists had to offer evidence to the scientific community that their position on the origins of life was just as probable as that of the evolutionists.

# CHAPTER 4

# The Battle for Scientific Legitimacy

Could it be that mainstream science had made an enormous mistake? Had humans and dinosaurs walked the Earth at the same time? Was the Earth actually billions of years younger than what was being taught in America's schools? Was there really no ancestral relationship between humans and other mammals? If there had been evolutionary development, could its progress at least have been guided by the wisdom of God?

In the years after the Creation Research Society was formed, certain Fundamentalist thinkers began devoting their lives to finding an answer to these questions. As a way of guiding them, Larry Butler, who was chair of the research committee, set some goals for future researchers.[1]

- Experimental demonstration that coal can be formed rapidly by catastrophes. This would disprove the idea that it had taken about 300 million years to form coal. Disproving it would give creationists a better chance to demonstrate that the fossils were much younger than evolutionists claimed they are.

- Experiments to form fossils under a variety of conditions to show that fossilization can take place relatively rapidly.
- Investigating coral reef formation and the stalactites of caves, mine shafts, and tunnels in hopes of proving that these geological formations can form more rapidly than most geologists think.
- Measuring variations in the thickness and shape of living human skulls. This might prove that some of the humanlike fossil skull shapes and thicknesses that evolutionists associated with human ancestors were instead contemporary variations.
- Determining what the global effects of a worldwide flood might be in order to give scientific validity to the idea of the Great Flood.
- Experimenting with soaking seeds in sea water to determine if some could survive a saltwater flood
- Studying the settling rates of different kinds of particles in water as a way to account for the order of fossils in the geological column.
- Reinvestigating the role heredity plays in development of various species of animals and plants
- Further research into how radioactive decay works—in order to point up possible mistakes in radioactive carbon dating.

Soon after these goals were laid out, creationists began flooding the *Creation Research Society Quarterly* with papers. The papers came from all over the country. Some of the writers had respected credentials in science and religion studies. Some had good credentials in the study of religion but questionable credentials in science; and some had neither. In fact, a disturbing number of the papers were so implausible that the editors refused to publish them. Occasionally, this led to bitter disputes.

It was clear from the start that there would never be much of a dialogue between scientists who believed in evolution and those who thought of themselves as literal creationists. The Creation Research Society's members had hoped that the *Creation Research Society Quarterly* would raise their status in the eyes of the scientific establishment, but their papers were rarely taken seriously by anyone except conservative Christians. Evolutionists who worked for mainstream scientific organizations were too busy investigating their own hypotheses. They often didn't even bother to counter creationist arguments against their ideas. The two positions continued to develop as two separate entities, with very little communication between them.

Nevertheless, the creationist scientists plowed on with more and more zeal, accumulating data they said proved the Genesis story. Two favorite targets of the creationist researchers were geology and the writings of Darwin. Perhaps their biggest challenge was to combat the massive amounts of evidence for evolution provided by the Grand Canyon. This deep chasm in northwestern Arizona, which has been cut out by the Colorado River, is thought to be about a million years old. The rocks in the lowest of its nine strata are thought to be much, much older. Most scientists think they date back to Precambrian times, from half a billion to a billion years ago. For the geologist or paleontologist, the Grand Canyon is a dream come true. It is like having the geologic column in cross section.

Many creationists think that the Grand Canyon strata are not nearly as old as most scientists claim. If they can prove themselves right, then they will have made some headway in their battle against the evolutionist's interpretation of the geologic column. The creationists' goal is to demonstrate that many of the fossils in the geological column are not those of animals or plants that lived during

*Geologists view the strata of the Grand Canyon as an almost perfect example of the geologic column, in which each layer represents a unit of time stretching back millions and sometimes billions of years. It is the most difficult mass of evidence for evolution that creationists must counter.*

various eras separated by millions of years, but animals and plants that were probably all created at the same time.

As an example of the creationist attack on conventional geology, consider a paper presented in 1994 in the *Creation Research Society Quarterly*[2] on massive flooding that had occurred in the Midwest the previous summer. According to the author, the Midwest floods proved that erosion of earth and rocks can occur very rapidly. He cited several locations where large quantities of rushing water from the Midwest floods had carved deep ruts in the Earth in a matter of days and had deposited several layers of mud and silt. He was suggesting that chasms like the Grand Canyon may have been created much less gradually than is believed. Perhaps the canyon had been carved out by the Great Flood, or maybe it was the result of other early catastrophes. The point of the paper was that such formations could come into being nearly at once. He left it to other creationist researchers to extend the hypothesis, hoping that one day it would lead to the certainty that the geologic column is not a record of millions of years of life on Earth but the record of a moment in history.

Another way for creationists to try to discredit the geologic column was to attack its fossil anomalies. Anomalies are exceptions to the order of fossils in strata. There were, for example, some claims by creationist Clifford Burdick about human skeletons found in Moab, Utah, in rock strata said to be 100 million years old. If this was true, it contradicted accepted ideas about modern humans, whom most evolutionists think first existed only about 2 million years ago. Creationists also insisted they had received reports about fossil human footprints in very old strata in Kentucky and in Utah. Those in Utah were supposedly found in the same strata as the fossils of trilobites, which most evolutionists say became extinct millions of years before humans existed.[3] The value in such claims for creationists lay in establishing the simultaneous existence of humans and supposedly more ancient prehistoric life forms. Even if they could not prove that the strata were not very, very old, they could still offer evidence for simultaneous creation of all life. They might, in the end, have to admit that life has existed on this planet for more than a few thousand years; but they held onto the premise that all life forms were created in their present form at nearly the same moment.

Some creationists began studying the tiny fossils of pollen and spores. Clifford Burdick, who claimed to have discovered the human skeletal remains in Moab, Utah, wrote about some fossil pollen he had found in Grand Canyon strata that mainstream scientists claimed were several hundred million years old. This was millions of years before the first pollen-producing plants were ever supposed to have existed.[4]

In his zeal to prove the Bible infallible, Burdick also began searching for clues about Noah's ark. He visited Mount Ararat, in northeastern Turkey, in 1996, where some creationists believe the ark finally came to rest. Although he really did not find any relics of an ark, he nevertheless maintained that the limestone found in the area was the exact age of what would have been deposited at the time of the Flood.[5]

A researcher named George Howe concentrated on trying to convince scientists that the Great Flood could have happened and that the ancestors of today's plants could have survived it. Howe soaked the seeds of fruit plants of five different species in sea water, tap water, or an equal mixture of both for a maximum of 140 days, which is roughly the time period given in the Bible for the Flood. He determined that some seeds could survive this maximum soaking period. To counter the objection that every type of seed is not that hardy, he insisted on the hypothesis that other seeds might have been protected inside the carcasses of birds that had eaten them or been frozen in icebergs until the Great Flood was over.[6]

In spearheading their attack on Darwin, creationists began reinterpreting his findings regarding the Galapagos Islands finches. Many creationists are comfortable with the idea of slight developmental changes within a species. It does not bother them to admit that finches might be born with a variety of beaks that make it more or less easy for them to find food within a particular environment. However, most creationists are uneasy with the idea that one species can develop into another or that more than one species can be descended from a common ancestor. The idea of one species developing into another contradicts the idea of a creation carefully planned and systematized by a supreme being. This supreme being is supposed to have created each species in the form in which it exists today. Then he created humans to rule over all other life forms.

The creationists were willing to grant that the Galapagos Islands finches may have changed. But they were eager to point out that all still remained *birds*. Neither the "molecule-to-man" concept of evolution nor the idea that all bird species arose from a common ancestor could be proven by such evidence. They also insisted that mutation played no part in the development of finches with differently shaped beaks. Some hypothesized that the population arrived from the mainland with all of the genes necessary to produce the variations. They believed that all of these genetic potentials were probably implanted in the first finches by God.[7]

The idea of a helpful mutated gene suddenly occurring later and by chance in finches is offensive to some creationists. Creationist Margaret J. Helder, in an article entitled "Let's Rewrite the Book on the Galapagos Islands,"[8] claimed that Darwin and those who came after him never admitted that the finches probably don't live in totally isolated populations. According to the Darwinian model, the finches came as a group with one gene pool, then were divided up on separate islands. Mutations arising in each separate population were favorable to some finches and led to new types of development. But Helder maintained that there must have been a lot of flying back and forth between the nearby islands. Thus, the populations weren't really isolated, which means that studies that assumed they were are all incorrect. New varieties of finches were not caused by mutations, she claimed, but by further crossbreeding of the original types that existed on the islands.

## CREATIONISTS AND HUMAN EVOLUTION

Another special target of the creationists is the evidence for human evolution. Creationists want every explanation of human origins to match up with biblical descriptions.

And they know that evolutionists can be made to look most vulnerable when it comes to that vague moment when our apelike ancestors were supposed to have developed into humans. The evidence for this transformation is not complete, and recent fossil discoveries that come close to documenting it are open to interpretation.

Creationist writings strive to prove that humans are no less recent on this planet than other creatures. The report of human footprint fossils in ancient rock strata described above was one way of doing this. Reinterpreting the human-like fossil finds of evolutionists was another. The creationists poked fun at fossils purported to be those of recent human ancestors. They either claimed that the fossil bones were really those of apes or insisted that they were not significantly different from the bones of some humans living today.

In their efforts to prove divine activity responsible for differences among humans, creationists have tried to forge a biblically sound, scientific account of the development of human races. Most evolutionists believe that the different races developed slowly over a long period of time. But creationists tend to think that the process was more like what is told in the biblical story of the Tower of Babel. In that story,

*Creationists cite the biblical story of the Tower of Babel as the explanation for the existence of the various cultural groups that inhabit the Earth.*

humans are presented as originally all speaking the same language. Then, they collaborate to build a tower high enough to reach Heaven. God is insulted by their arrogance and transforms their single tongue into many. Immediately after, since they can no longer communicate with each other, each language group goes its different way. Over a few generations, they develop into the different races of the world.

Creationist R. Daniel Shaw[9] suggested that God may have bestowed a different language on each group based upon genetic similarities. After Babel, as each group became isolated, inbreeding within each accentuated these genetic characteristics, leading to the development of separate races. As proof of this hypothesis, he collected data about the blood types of indigenous populations on the South Pacific island of New Guinea in 37 areas distributed over the entire island. From the blood tests, he discovered that, near as they were to each other, these population areas tended to be isolated genetically. In addition, each had developed its own specific language and culture. Shaw's purpose was to construct a model of race origin showing how God divided up humanity into populations of different physical characteristics. He thought this could have happened fairly rapidly and with populations that were initially close to each other, as demonstrated by the New Guinea example.

Shaw was one of many creationists who hoped to draw people to their cause by placing familiar religious parables in a scientific context. These efforts succeeded in some cases. Americans who supported the views in the Bible but who were also conscious of the great advances in scientific inquiry made during the century were attracted by this blend of creationism and the scientific method. However, creationists would soon find that the scientific establishment did not take much notice of their challenges. Most evolutionists preferred to devote their energies to conducting further research into the origins of life rather than to combating the creationist cause.

# CHAPTER 5

# Contemporary Research and Controversy

As stated before, most evolutionist writings do not concentrate on refuting or confirming creationist claims. Instead of spending their time examining fossils that are supposed to be human footprints or soaking seeds in salt water, evolutionists keep busy gathering more and more evidence for their own hypotheses. These hypotheses are, in general, based upon the work of Darwin and Mendel. Usually it is the creationists who are on the defensive and who must define themselves by refuting the positions of the evolutionists. Most of their writings have to refer to the famous evolutionist theories that they are trying to prove or disprove. Among evolutionists, however, most controversies are internal. They center around interpretations of Darwinian concepts. Evolutionist theorists and researchers are busy refining their position on Darwin or opposing the detailed views of another Darwinian. Most agree that the work needed to prove evolution is far from over.

In general, most evolutionists have the same basic assumptions as other mainstream scientists. Although some may believe that life's origins and developments have been guided by a divine creator, this is not the subject of their study. They believe that supernatural questions are simply out of their realm. A 1981 statement from the

National Academy of Sciences has gone so far as to say, "Religion and science are separate and mutually exclusive realms of human thought whose presentation in the same context leads to a misunderstanding of both scientific theory and religious belief." Another basic difference between evolutionist scientists and creationist scientists is that most creationist scientists subscribe to Bacon's theories of inductive reasoning. They are busy collecting evidence that might conflict with evolution or finding holes in evolutionary theory. And their own theories rely heavily on supernatural explanations of phenomena, which they consider a reasonable area of inquiry.

One should also keep in mind that there are some antievolutionists who are not traditional creationists. Various scientific books, such as Michael Denton's *Evolution: A Theory in Crisis,* have tried to disprove that natural selection is the key factor in evolutionary development. Writer Arthur Koestler, linguistics expert Noam Chomsky, and science historian Stanley Jaki have also denied some of the basic tenets of evolutionary theory, but none of these people believe in creationism, either.[1]

In recent years new studies have both enlarged the original scope of evolution and modified some of its assertions. Some of the studies take new looks at old data. For example, one of the classic examples of observable natural selection is the story of the English pepper moth. In the late 1800s, English factories spewed smoke into the environment, killing the grayish lichen that covered trees. At that time, the English pepper moth had salt-and-pepper-colored wings that provided perfect camouflage whenever the moth rested upon a surface covered in lichen. But as the lichen disappeared because of pollution and tree trunks were coated with black soot from the factories, the salt-and-pepper-colored moths could be easily spotted by predatory birds, or so it was assumed. The moths more likely to survive these conditions

*The color changes in the English pepper moth population over time have provided evolutionary scientists with documented evidence of natural selection.*

seemed to be the very few that were completely black. In a relatively short time, the population changed. Now black moths predominated, and the salt-and-pepper moths nearly disappeared. At the time and until recently, scientists thought this was because the dark moths had better camouflage. When factories modernized and clean-air laws were passed in Britain in the 1950s, the situation was reversed. It became easier for salt-and-pepper moths to survive. Meanwhile, almost all the black-colored moths died out.

The story of the pepper moths is a favorite way of illustrating evolution in beginning biology books. But it was only recently that scientists began discussing data on the same phenomenon in a different part of the world.[2] According to reports, pepper moths in Michigan went through the same changes. By 1959, the dark moths outnumbered all others in polluted areas of Detroit. But after 1963, when the U.S. adopted clean-air laws, the salt-and-pepper variety returned.

The two studies are very important to evolutionists because they document the same evolutionary process in different locales. It is like being able to try the same experiment a second time. Evolutionists are pointing to the close similarities as proof of the doctrine of natural selection. As long as the environmental conditions for an organism are fairly similar, one can expect the same process of adaptation over generations. However, there are holes in the classic explanation of the phenomenon of the moths. Evolutionists had always assumed that the disappearance and return of the lichen, and its effect upon the camouflage ability of the moths, produced the changes. It turns out, however, that the light forms of the moth returned before the lichen came back in England, and in Detroit the lichen never really disappeared, despite the increase in pollution. It now seems that the dark moths were better adapted to a polluted environment for some other reason, but that reason has not yet been pinpointed.

Creationists love to point out inconsistencies, uncertainties, and disagreements in the evolution camp. Several have cited a famous evolutionary biologist from Harvard who they think has made some statements that support their point of view. His name is Stephen Jay Gould and he is known for his innovative thinking in the field of evolution. Gould has stated that he does not think natural selection always plays a role at some of the highest levels of evolution, such as creation of a species. He maintains that other stronger or more sudden forces may be at work.[3]

In 1972 Niles Eldredge, of the American Museum of Natural History, and Gould introduced a new theory called punctuated equilibrium. According to the theory, the fossil record cannot be read as a tale of gradual, continuous evolutionary change, as Darwin had suggested. Instead, there are long periods without change that are punctuated by busy bursts of change during which new species are

*Harvard biologist Stephen Jay Gould (right) poses with Nobel laureate in chemistry Christian Afinsen (left) and UC-Davis geneticist Francisco Ayala (center). The men were three of seventy-two leaders in science who signed a letter to the Supreme Court in protest of Louisiana's creation science statute.*

formed.[4] What is more, some of the important changes that we associate with the development of species may not have been guided by natural selection. They may be merely side effects of the process. For example, most insects are small because an external skeleton can only accommodate a certain body size. Thus, their smallness is probably a side effect of having an external skeleton and is not an adaptation to environmental factors.

For some creationists, the theory of punctuated equilibrium is a near-admission that the biblical theory of instantaneous creation might be right. If other forces outside of natural selection are responsible for change, then maybe those other powerful forces referred to are the will of God in which creationists believe. And if dramatic changes in species could occur very rapidly and are not dependent upon natural selection, then maybe the story of God creating new life forms in a single day is closer to the truth than many would expect.

However, in the years that followed the announcement of Eldredge's and Gould's new theory, Gould made it clear that it was in no way an endorsement of the creationist position. Gould does believe that mass extinctions of species probably have occurred, but he does not think that the most important of these mass extinctions was caused by any flood resembling the one described in Genesis. Also, the periods of rapid change to which Gould is referring are certainly not nearly as rapid as most creationists would like them to be. He thinks the changes took place over thousands or tens of thousands of years.

As a matter of fact, another aspect of Gould's evolutionary philosophy is totally at odds with creation philosophy. He believes that the story of evolution is not a story of progressively improved organisms leading up to the glory that is the human being. It is instead a series of random and chaotic events that are linked together into a pattern. Gould is quick to disappoint any notions of humans as the lords of all creation. If, he reasons, a small, unimportant group of ancient fishes had not evolved fin bones with a strong central axis, then vertebrates may never have become land dwelling. If the dinosaurs had not been wiped off the face of the Earth by a large comet or asteroid that struck about 65 million years ago, then mammals would never have been able to compete with them. And finally, if a small group of primates in Africa had not developed upright posture, then our ancestors might have developed into apes, rather than humans.[5] In other words, as Gould says, "We're latecomers on this planet, while the bacteria have been around forever and probably will still be here when the sun explodes."[6] Gould goes so far as to say:

> Homo sapiens did not appear on the earth, just a geologic second ago, because evolutionary theory predicts such an outcome based on themes of progress and increasing neural complexity. Humans arose, rather, as a fortuitous and contingent outcome of thousands of linked events, any one of which could have occurred differently and sent history on an alternative pathway that would not have led to consciousness.[7]

Evolutionary theories claiming that chance factors lead to changes in species directly contradict the creationist idea of world events planned and guided by an all-knowing God, whom some people call an "intelligent designer." Still, not all of today's evolutionists believe that evolution is the product of chance. Some tend to see a very strict pattern in its workings. Recently, a team of biologists restaged the evolution of a species of sunflower known as the anomalous sunflower, or *Helianthus anomalus*.[8] The anomalous sunflower is the hybrid product of two other sunflower species. Researchers bred these two species to see how similar their offspring would be to today's anomalous sunflowers. If chance ruled in the evolution of the *anomalus*, then the hybrids the researchers produced might not all be similar to it. But in every case they were. The researchers reasoned that the hybrids all ended up alike because certain combinations of genes from the two parent sunflowers work together better than others. In other words, the genetic future of the new species followed predictable patterns, given similar starting conditions, environment, and other factors.

# THE ORIGINS OF LIFE

Lively disputes have arisen over many of the finer points of evolution, but few issues are as touchy as those dealing with the actual beginnings of life. It is an issue that automatically brings up the question of whether or not there is a God. For those who feel certain that there is one, the issue becomes how much of an active part God has played in life's origins and development. Opinions range from the biblical, in which God instantaneously creates life as we now know it, to the biochemical, in which God is seen as responsible for creating certain chemicals whose reactions synthesized the first protein compounds and enzymes. These compounds and enzymes eventually became the first living organisms.

For those who think there is no God, the question is restricted to the chemical. What chance occurrences created certain chemical reactions that first synthesized the protein building blocks and enzymes of living things? Such people must by necessity avoid the question of who or what created the universe in order that the chemical reactions could occur. However, they might answer such a difficulty by saying that those who believe in God also avoid the issue of first cause, because they can never explain who created God.

Many evolutionists would say that questions about the origin of life are beyond the scope of evolution, or at least are not purely Darwinian issues. But what mainstream scientists think about the origin of life is of interest to this discussion because the subject is so often brought up by dissenting creationists. Current scientific theory maintains that about 4.6 billion years ago, our planet was covered with molten rock that was constantly showered with meteorites. Frequent chemical reactions produced proteins and enzymes, some of which eventually organized into the molecules that make up living things. About 4 billion years ago, the surface of the Earth cooled down enough to support chains of unicellular organisms called cyanobacteria, or blue-green algae, that resemble today's pond scum. It took another 2 billion years for cells with nuclei to evolve. Complex multicellular organisms took even longer.

In October 1995, some Chinese geologists reported that they had found evidence suggesting that complex living things originated much earlier than most researchers thought.[9] Digging in northern China, the researchers found more than 300 leaflike fossils that probably lived on the ocean floor about 1.7 billion years ago. The fossils resembled a kind of multicellular plant thought to have lived 700 million years later and supposed to be the earliest multicellular life form.

Meanwhile, other researchers may have found the earliest known representative of the chordates, the branch of the animal kingdom to which vertebrates, including humans, belong.[10] This early member of the chordates is a 525-million-year-old fossil that resembles a fish and possesses a notochord, an organ from which the spinal column developed. Most people had thought that chordates developed much later—around 430 million years ago. The earlier date means that chordates are associated with a host of earlier animal forms and may not be a special product of later evolution. In hearing the news, Stephen Jay Gould remarked, "So much for chordate uniqueness marked by slightly later evolution. As for our place in the history of life, we are of it, not above it."

## HUMAN EVOLUTION

Among evolutionists, ideas about human origins can be almost as controversial as they are for creationists. Most creationists tend to shun any theory that suggests that there were certain evolutionary stages leading back from modern humans to nonhuman ancestors. As far as they are concerned, the very first human beings, Adam and Eve, were identical to us in structure and function. They had no ancestors and were the direct result of God's creation. On the other hand, evolutionists all tend to agree that humans evolved from an apelike ancestor, but they have conflicting opinions about the various stages in this process. These opinions are revised with each new discovery, and there are likely to be more discoveries in the future.

In 1891, fossil remains thought to have belonged to an ancestor of modern humans who lived a million years ago were found in Java and dubbed "Java Man." Since then, other fossil discoveries have filled in the periods before and after Java Man, but the picture is far from complete. The general agreement among evolutionists in the scientific community is that humans today belong to a primate species known as *Homo sapiens* and that human ancestry can be traced back to early hominids about 4 or 5 million years ago.

Creationists such as Duane Gish, a spokesman for the Institute for Creation Research, insist that Java Man and other fossils like it are really those of an ancient ape that has nothing to do with the history of the human species.[11] As support Gish quotes a book written in 1921 and revised in 1957 by French scientists Marcellin Boule and Henri Vallois. Using material from the same book, which many evolutionists consider to be out of date, Gish has tried to prove that another fossil of the same species, known as Peking Man, is also an ape. His general position is that all of the humanlike fossils that have been discovered are nonhuman or else the fossils of modern humans.

To oppose evolutionists, Gish points to the case of Piltdown Man, a fossil that was really a hoax that had been constructed from fragments of a human skull and an orangutan's jaw. Then there was Nebraska Man, a single tooth that was later proved to have come from an extinct pig. Finally, there was Orce Man, from Spain, which was

*This side view of the skullcap of Java Man shows the protruding brow ridge typical of* Homo erectus, *considered by most evolutionists to be a direct ancestor of modern humans.*

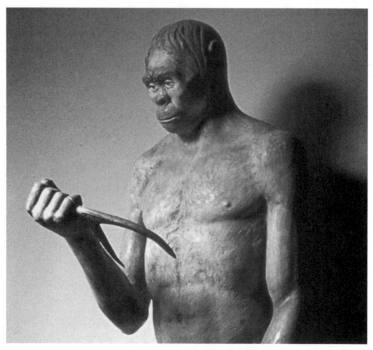

*This reconstruction of Java Man as he might have looked in life was made by a Dutch anatomist based on fossil skeletal material.*

later proved to be a fragment of the skull of a donkey.[12] However, these hoaxes were long ago revealed as such by evolutionists themselves.

In 1984 Gish was asked to explain why the evolutionary findings of molecular biology agree so closely with those of anatomy.[13] Molecular biologists have discovered that some key sequences of amino acids in humans and chimpanzees are identical, whereas humans and more distant animals, such as the frog, have much less similar sequences of amino acids. They reasoned that the closer the sequences of amino acids are to each other, the more likely the organisms are to have descended from a common ancestor. In a PBS interview on the program "Nova," Gish countered that scientists were only looking selectively at the amino acid chains. If they were to look at data for other proteins, they might find, for example, that humans and frogs also had some identical chains. Since no one else could find the proteins to which Gish was referring, they challenged him to come up with documentation. None of this documentation has been provided by him.

Most evolutionists now group humans, the African apes, and the extinct ancestors of humans in the same family, which is called the Hominidae. The human line in this family, separate from the ape line, is called the Homininae, or hominines. The distinction clears up a popular misconception about human evolution that has flourished in the media since the Scopes trial. Humans are not thought to be descended from apes, as journalists during the Scopes trial often suggested. Instead, humans and apes are like two prongs on the same fork; both subfamilies are descended from a long-ago common ancestor.

Hominines are distinguished from other Hominidae by their ability to walk on two legs, their ability to make tools, and their larger braincase. As humans evolved, there was a change in the shape of the face and the teeth. Teeth became smaller and did not protrude as much from the

*Evolutionary theorists believe that humans and apes descended from a common ancestor who lived many millions of years ago, and they thus group all the various species into the family Hominidae.*

mouth. The face dropped below the brain case instead of projecting out in front of it.

There are gaps in the very early records of human evolution, and one of them has to do with the links between apelike animals who lived in Africa between 7 and 20 million years ago and the human subfamily. Plenty of fossils of these early creatures have been found, but nothing definitely links them to those hypothesized Hominidae from which humans are thought to be descended.

Most evolutionists think that the very first fossil evidence for the subgroup that became the ancestors of humans is *Australopithecus,* examples of which were discovered in eastern and southern Africa. Several species of *Australopithecus* seem to have existed as long as 4 or 5 million years ago and then become extinct about 1.5 million years ago. Some *Australopithecus* fossils have a brain size that was slightly larger than that of chimpanzees. Later versions no longer had protruding teeth, but no *Australopithecus* is associated with the use of tools. However, some scientists think that hominines separated from the ape line even earlier than *Australopithecus*—as long as 7 million years ago.

About 2.6 million years ago, while Australopithecus still roamed the Earth, there may have been as many as four different species of hominines. One species of hominine apparently evolved into the genus *Homo*, which in turn finally evolved into modern humans. The other species of hominines became extinct. Early fossils of the genus *Homo* are varied and dated back to about 1.5 million years ago. Then in 1996, the discovery of an upper jaw in northern Ethiopia extended the *Homo* genus back some 2.3 million years.[14]

Some of the early members of the genus *Homo* have large brain cases but also retained their large, apelike teeth. Others have small teeth and small brain cases. Some of the fossils are associated with stone tool manufacture. Whether these early tool users are really the ancestors of humans has never been established without a doubt, but many specialists in human evolution believe that they are.

Fossils of a large-brained, small-toothed variety of *Homo* have been found in Kenya and date back from 1.5 to 1.6 million years ago. More complicated tools are associated with this species, which is called *Homo erectus*. *Erectus* refers to the fact that most of these individuals stood upright. They also used fire and hunted large animals.

Until recently, most evolutionists were also fairly certain that the first upright member of the Hominidae developed way before *Homo erectus*, around 3.7 million years ago. This idea is based on the discovery of footprints embedded in volcanic ash in Tanzania. Some were surprised in 1995 when researchers discovered a fossil of a 4.4- million-year-old hominid in Ethiopia and a 4.2-million year-old hominid in Kenya.[15] Both seem to have had the ability to walk upright as well. These new species were more apelike than any hominids that had been discovered before, but they could walk.

Most evolutionists believe that a fairly clear development can be traced through the later descendants of *Homo erectus*, based roughly on increasing brain sizes. This finally resulted in a new species called *Homo sapiens*, or "thinking man," about 200,000 to 300,000 years ago, the species to which we belong. However, once again, the fossil record is murky. Many scientists insist that no unbroken evolutionary development between the first *Homo sapiens* and modern humans can be traced. The dispute over this centers around a group of *Homo sapiens* known as Neanderthals, whose fossils were first found in the Neander Valley in Germany. They seem to have lived in Europe and the Middle East from 100,000 years ago to

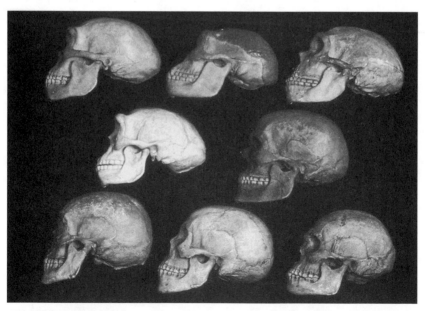

*These skulls exemplify various stages in human evolution. The most primitive skulls are on top, and a modern human skull is at bottom right.*

about 35,000 or 40,000 years ago. But suddenly they disappear from the fossil record, and their connection to modern humans is still hotly debated.

## An Attack on Creationists by an Evolutionist

There isn't, in fact, one reputable evolutionist who would insist that every detail of the story of human development has been accounted for by science. And such doubts are exactly what creationists rely upon. They rush to adapt each new fossil discovery to a biblical interpretation. They claim that the mysterious gaps in the fossil record are evidence that the generally accepted interpretation of it is wrong. Occasionally, a well-known member of the scientific establishment attempts to answer their accusations.

In 1996, astronomer Carl Sagan published a book called *The Demon-Haunted World: Science as a Candle in the Dark*. In it, Sagan lumped creationists with pseudoscientists, whose superstitions he felt were a danger to the future of an educated world. Sagan referred to national polls showing that 57 percent of Americans think that dinosaurs were still living when humans evolved. He said that about half of the American populace believes that the Earth was created about 10,000 years ago and that the dinosaurs disappeared during the Flood because they were too big to fit on the ark. His book is a scathing indictment not just of the creationists, but of anyone who relies on supernatural explanations for phenomena, from astrologers to Christian Scientists. To counter the objection that without the supernatural, existence would lose its awe and wonder, Sagan points to what he considers some wondrous truths of legitimate science, such as the fact that we are made of atoms that may have originated all over the universe.

The fact that about half of all Americans still believe in a young Earth and in dinosaurs coexisting with humans should hearten creationists. It is proof that despite changes in American education, a large proportion of people, at least when questioned, still accept traditional biblical ways of looking at the development of life. However, since the new BSCS biology books of the 1960s, creationists have felt the need to exert a less casual influence on the thinking of America's young people. And it has become clear to them that all the creationist research in the world may not be enough to sway future minds.

Realizing this early on, a committee of the Creation Research Society decided to write a creationist high school biology textbook called *Biology: The Search for Order in Complexity*, which was published by a small Christian publisher in 1970. Although the first 10,000 copies sold fairly quickly, only a few public schools adopted the book. When one school district in southern Indiana decided to use it as the sole textbook for its biology curriculum, a state court promptly banned it from use in public schools.[16]

In the years that followed, there were other creationists textbook projects. They tended to stress scientific reasoning over literal interpretation of the Bible and often did not directly attack evolution. Instead they presented philosophical discussions about the patterns of development of various life forms, hoping gently to lead the student toward the realization that the world was the product of an "intelligent designer."

Despite these efforts, it was still evident to a lot of creationists that their research, publishing, and education efforts just weren't enough. Many began thinking that real power lay in the changing of local and state laws, or at least in influencing the decisions made by school boards. In the last couple of decades, the forefront of the creation-evolution battle has turned away from high-profile state laws and moved toward local legislatures and communities.

CHAPTER 6

# Court Confrontations
# and Local Skirmishes

Anyone who reads newspapers or watches television today knows creationists have succeeded in making their voices heard. To do so, they've launched a three-pronged attack on evolution that has made use of state legislatures, the courts, and individual communities and school boards. One of the most startling early incidences of this activism took place in 1974 in Kanawha County, West Virginia.[1] That year an outraged member of the school board, Alice Moore, called for the banning of 175 books that had been chosen as part of a language arts program. The school board had chosen the books because they thought that they emphasized the many contributions that minorities have made to American growth and culture. However, Moore and her supporters were convinced that the books were an abomination to any well-meaning Christian.

The books that so offended Moore and other parents encouraged students to discuss many of the issues that young people must face today, such as drug and alcohol addiction, sex, urban violence, politics, and patriotism. Moore and her colleagues went so far as to accuse the books of sanctioning dangerous and immoral behavior. She said the books were "filthy, trashy, disgusting, one-sidedly in favor of blacks, and unpatriotic."[2] Kanawha

*Alice Moore, a minister's wife, led a campaign to ban 175 books chosen as part of the language arts curriculum in the Kanawha County schools in West Virginia. Moore and other conservative parents considered the books immoral and un-Christian, in part, because some taught evolution as a fact.*

County is home to Charleston, the state capital, but the rest of the county consists of small, rural communities that are mostly white and Protestant. It may be that all the issues presented in the books were not that relevant to life in Kanawha County. However, Moore also had one other outraged complaint against the books. She cited certain passages that she said presented evolution as if it were a fact.

After appearing on television, Moore convinced the local PTA to vote against allowing several of the books in school on the grounds that they were anti-American and devoid of moral ideas. When the board adopted the books anyway, about 10,000 parents kept their children home from school in protest. In addition, they picketed

businesses throughout the county and kept school and city buses from operating on their routes.[3]

Eventually, disagreements reached the point of random gunfire and vandalism of school property. Some schools were even firebombed. What is more, the mayor of one town who supported the protesters had the superintendent and some board members arrested for contributing to the delinquency of minors because they would not ban the books.[4]

After compromises on both sides, the incident died down. However, some say it was instrumental in strengthening an already-existing textbook-banning movement among conservative Christians across the country. Complaints about biology textbooks adopted by the states of California and Texas were in full furor by the time of the Kanawha incident. Both of these states have "textbook adoption" policies. That means that periodically a committee decides which textbooks will be used throughout the entire state. In California, disagreements about evolution content in biology books turned into a struggle between creationists and evolutionists that lasted more than two decades and is still not completely settled.

In the 1960s, passages in all California biology textbooks that discussed evolution had to be softened and made more neutral. Ideas were restated to make it apparent that evolution was no more than one of several theories. Meanwhile, in Texas, the only biology books that discussed evolution were stricken from an approved list. Later in the 1970s, books that did discuss evolution were allowed, but had to carry a disclaimer stating that evolution was a theory and not a fact. By the late 1980s and the 1990s, both states had backed down considerably, after concerted efforts by scientists and church-state-separation advocates, and evolution was back in textbooks and more strongly stated. However, individual school boards and teachers kept creationist ideas circulating throughout school systems.

# THE NEW CHRISTIAN RIGHT

The Kanawha incident and others like it were fueled by the values and activities of a new Religious Right, a loose coalition of conservative Protestants that has produced powerful political activists and a huge voting bloc within the last twenty-five years. This group also has ties to some conservative Catholic believers. The coalition now has strong allies in the Republican Party and a very active political agenda. In general, but not always, its goals include bringing prayer back into the schools, giving creationism equal time in textbooks, outlawing abortion and homosexual rights, fighting against big government and heavy taxes, and promoting family values. The Christian Right promotes its values on television and in radio broadcasts throughout the country. Its members lobby government officials, run for government posts, fight court cases, and put pressure on and run for positions on school boards.

The growth of the Christian Right has partly accomplished what conservative Protestant ministers, intellectuals, and scientists have been trying to accomplish since the 1950s. Relying less on attempts at scientific proof and scholarly research, the Christian Right has used grassroots efforts and media campaigns to appeal to the hearts and minds of a good percentage of fundamentalist Christians. In 1987, 46 percent of adults polled disagreed with the statement, "Humans beings as we know them today developed form earlier species of animals."[5] Four years later, in 1991, a Gallup Poll found that 47 percent of Americans and 25 percent of all college graduates believed the statement, "God created man pretty much in his present form at one time within the last 10,000 years."[6] It's as if the potential supporters of the antievolution movement were merely waiting to be recruited. One should also keep in mind that opposition to evolution is only one small part of the agenda of the Christian Right.

When questions of sexual morality, patriotism, anticommunism, big government, and abortion are included with the package, the creationist agenda becomes part of a highly emotional set of issues. But who exactly is attracted by such a value package? From what segment of American society does the Christian Right come?

Today, members of the Christian Right are difficult to characterize. Most are avowed Evangelicals, spiritual descendants of the eighteenth-century Protestant movement that stressed one's personal relationship to Jesus Christ. (However, not all Evangelicals identify with the Christian Right.) The Evangelical movement has always called for preaching, outreach, and a strong moral code, but not all members of it are strict biblical literalists and not all of them are strict creationists. Traditionally, Evangelicals are associated with rural life and the working classes, but as far back as 15 years ago, many Evangelicals began moving into the middle-class mainstream and to urban areas.

In 1983, two sociologists, Stuart Rothenberg and Frank Newport, collected data about income, occupations, and other social factors relating to Evangelicals, or those people who categorize themselves as intense believers in Christianity. The results are shown in the table on page 84.

The statisticians found that, in many ways, a good percentage of Evangelicals were close to the population norm, but this was a bit less true for the segment that also believed that the Bible was literally true. The biblical literalists tended to be somewhat poorer and somewhat less educated than the general population. They also tended to be more conservative about such issues as abortion and women's rights. Of course, biblical literalists are also more likely to be creationists than any other type of Evangelical.

In more recent years, many Evangelicals have seen their incomes and educational levels increase. More now occupy managerial or professional positions. With their improved status has come increased political and economic power.

## Selected Demographic and Opinion Data on
## Evangelicals and "Biblical Literalists" 1983[*]

|  | U.S.Adults % | Evangelicals % | Biblical Literalists % |
|---|---|---|---|
| Females | 52 | 60 | 63 |
| College/graduate school graduates | 27 | 22 | 12 |
| Family income above $30,000 | 32 | 33 | 27 |
| White-collar occupation | n.a. | 35 | 28 |
| Age 55 or older | 24 | 32 | 40 |
| Favor voluntary prayer in public schools | 81 | 91 | n.a. |
| Think abortion should be illegal in all circumstances | 16 | 27 | 33 |
| Favor ERA | 59 | 56 | 55 |
| Usually vote Democratic | 43 | 47 | 50 |

[*] From Stuart Rothenberg and Frank Newport, *The Evangelical Voter: Religion and Politics in America.* Washington, D.C.: The Institute for Government and Politics in the Creationist Movement, 1984.

However, one could say that their values are still more closely connected to the American past than are the values of most Americans. For example, many strict Evangelicals view alcoholism, drug addiction, and some forms of mental illness in religious terms, rather than as mental or physical illnesses. They feel that a correct relationship with God and with the teachings of the Bible is more likely to cure addiction and some mental diseases than the best psychiatrists and doctors. This is a view of addiction and mental health that would be more likely to have been expressed in earlier centuries.

Many Evangelicals have a vision of Christianity as an intense, emotional experience. Some, such as certain Pentecostalist sects, believe in prophecy, speaking in tongues, and faith healing. All of these experiences, which lead to strong ideas about how to behave and how to accomplish one's goals, do not rely upon scientific verification to produce conviction. Belief is personal and internal, and belief is enough. Some strict Evangelicals may feel that their way of life, which has roots in the American past, is in danger of losing ground.[7] This may be why some have so effectively banded together into groups that intensely promote it.

The Christian Right, then, can be thought of as one segment of the larger contemporary Evangelical movement. And one of the most powerful of the New Christian Right's promotional groups is a faction called the Christian Coalition. It came together in 1989 after Pat Robertson, a television evangelist, lost a 1988 bid for the U.S. presidency. Mailing lists from the campaign helped him and others create an organization that had swelled to about 350,000 members by 1993 and that had strong links to the Republican Party. The Christian Coalition now has a full-time staff in 15 states, 750 local chapters across the United States, a Washington lobbyist, and a budget of several million dollars.[8]

*Christian Coalition founder Pat Robertson has been at the forefront of the Christian Right's rise to power in recent years. His grass roots political organization targets local school boards and other elected offices as entry points for conservative candidates.*

The Christian Coalition has claimed tax-exempt status as a religious-education organization, but this has not kept it from offering political training seminars and fund-raising campaigns to oppose such issues as the acceptance of homosexuals into the military. In 1991, Pat Robertson went so far as to tell his supporters, "We are training people to be effective—to be elected to school boards, to city councils, to state legislatures and to key positions in political parties. . . . By the end of this decade, if we work and give and organize and train, the Christian Coalition will be the most powerful political organization in America."[9]

# THE CHRISTIAN RIGHT
## AND LEGISLATION

The Christian Coalition is far from the first organization with a creationist political agenda. Long before its birth, some creationists pressured law makers to take steps to make creationism a sanctioned and socially accepted point of view. In 1973, their efforts influenced the Tennessee legislature to pass a law requiring all biology textbooks to identify evolution as a theory rather than as a scientific fact. The law also required that the Genesis account of life's origins be given equal space. The law was struck down in the courts in 1975 on the grounds that it mandated religious instruction in public schools. But a 1976 Kentucky law took a softer approach. It merely allowed teachers the option of presenting Genesis in addition to evolutionary theory. This law remains on the books.[10]

Meanwhile, some creation scientists were radically revising their attack on evolution. They had all but abandoned the idea of bringing creationism into the mainstream through the medium of established science. Their new goal was to make scientific creationism speak a language that could be understood and approved by the lawmakers. With this in mind, Wendell Bird,[11] a creationist and Yale Law School graduate, wrote a law article that would be used to forge propositions for state laws by several creationist lawmakers. It stated that teaching only evolution was a form of favoritism because it automatically sanctioned certain religious faiths and world views. It maintained that the support of evolution implied official disapproval of some religious beliefs and forced children to learn material that they and their families found unfriendly to their way of worship.

Bird recommended neutrality. This would mean teaching both evolution and creationism, which he maintained was also a science. Although his resolution was intended for the use of local school boards who wanted government permission to add creationism to the curriculum, another creationist named Paul Ellwanger,[12] who belonged to an organization named Citizens for Fairness in Education, modified Bird's ideas into a legislative bill that was introduced into several state legislatures in 1981. Most of these attempts at passing the bill died, but in 1981 two actually became laws. One, which is known as the Arkansas Law, led to a landmark case that affected the fate of the creationists for many years to come.

It's worth taking a detailed look at the Arkansas Law and what became of it. It brought the conflict between creationists and evolutionists to a head. The court decision that followed it in 1982, which is called *McLean v. Arkansas Board of Education,* became a model for most subsequent cases like it.

The new law was labeled Act 590 of 1981 and was entitled the "Balanced Treatment for Creation-Science and Evolution-Science Act."[13] As you can see, its very title gave official approval to the idea of creationism as a science. It defined creation science as "the scientific evidences for creation and inferences from those scientific evidences," which included "sudden creation of the universe, energy and life from nothing."[14] It had been based on a bill proposed by Ellwanger and introduced by a conservative state senator named James Holsted. Holsted had the support of the Greater Little Rock Evangelical Fellowship Committee and a group known as Family Life, America and God (FLAG). But the new bill was immediately challenged in federal court by the ACLU, the same organization that had been active in the Scopes trial. Joining with them was a coalition of Protestant, Catholic, and Jewish religious leaders, who felt that the law violated the First Amendment. These people were able to command a host of world-famous witnesses on behalf of evolution, including Stephen Jay Gould.[15]

The creationists, on the other hand, avoided inviting well-known Institute for Creation Research figures, such as Henry Morris and Duane Gish. At that point in time, the IRC was not very well respected by either the scientific establishment or the media. The defenders of the bill relied instead on the testimony of Harold Coffin of the Geoscience Research Institute and, among others, even called upon non-Christian mathematician Chandra Wickramasinghe, mainly because he disagreed with most established scientists on the origin of life.[16]

The verdict by Judge William R. Overton is one of the most complete overviews of the creation-evolution debate available today. The judge's purpose was to determine whether or not the law interfered with the "establishment of religion" clause of the First Amendment, which affirms, "Neither a state nor the Federal Government can set up a church. Neither can pass laws which aid one religion, aid all religions, or prefer one religion over another."[17]

In part two of the verdict, Judge Overton provided a history of the controversy, explaining the beginnings of the Fundamentalist movement in America in the nineteenth century, mentioning the crisis in science education caused by *Sputnik* and the BSCS textbooks, and describing the birth of scientific creationism following publication of *The Genesis Flood*. The judge also showed a far-reaching understanding of the scope of the conflict by quoting a passage from *The Bible Has the Answer* by Henry Morris and Martin E. Clark, which said:

> Evolution is thus not only anti-Biblical and anti-Christian, but it is utterly unscientific and impossible as well. But it has served effectively as the pseudo-scientific basis of atheism, agnosticism, socialism, fascism, and numerous other false and dangerous philosophies over the past century.

Once the judge had established how creationists seem to hold evolution responsible for other evils, he maintained that the creationist organizations that supported the bill "consider the introduction of creation science into the public schools part of their ministry." To prove this, he mentioned two pamphlets published by the Institute for Creation Research that offered methods of convincing school boards, administrators, and teachers to allow creationism to be taught in public schools.

To offer more proof that this particular bill was part of creationist religious activism, the judge focused on the involvement of Ellwanger's group Citizens for Fairness in Education in passing the bill. He said that Ellwanger's views on creation science had to be looked at since he had forged the model act upon which Act 590 was based. He quoted a letter that Ellwanger had written to a pastor in which he stated, "While neither evolution nor creation can qualify as a scientific theory, and since it is virtually impossible at this point to educate the whole world that evolution is not a true scientific theory, we have freely used these terms—the evolution theory and the theory of scientific creationism—in the bill's text."

According to the judge, Ellwanger's writings showed that he was aware that Act 590 was "a religious crusade, coupled with a desire to conceal this fact." He even quoted another letter that Ellwanger wrote to a Florida state senator in which he cautioned, "It would be very wise, if not actually essential, that all of us who are engaged in this legislative effort be careful not to present our position and our work in a religious framework." What is more, Ellwanger had testified,

> I'm trying to play on [people's] emotions, love, hate, their likes, dislikes, because I don't know any other way to involve, to get humans to become involved in human endeavors. . . . I

believe that the predominance of the population in America that represents the greatest potential for taking some kind of action in this area is a Christian community.

By making such statements, Ellwanger demonstrated an evangelical attitude that had more to do with efforts at emotionally moving and influencing Christian believers than it had to do with supporting the balanced treatment of two scientific theories. Or at least, that is what Judge Overton concluded. In his words, "the State failed to produce any evidence which would warrant an inference or conclusion that at any point in the process anyone considered the legitimate educational value of the Act. It was simply and purely an effort to introduce the Biblical version of creation into the public school curricula. The only inference which can be drawn from these circumstances is that the Act was passed with the specific purpose by the General Assembly of advancing religion."

As proof that creationism wasn't science, regardless of the motives of those who had developed the bill, Judge Overton listed the essential characteristics of science:

1. It is guided by natural law.
2. It has to be explanatory by reference to natural law.
3. It is testable against the empirical world.
4. Its conclusions are tentative, i.e., are not necessarily the final word.
5. It is falsifiable (meaning, that it has the potential to be proved wrong by testing).

He maintained that creation science did not live up to these standards. In the first place, the theory of creation revolved around a sudden creation "from nothing." This concept depended upon supernatural forces that were not guided by "natural" law. And the hypothesis of creation from nothing couldn't be tested or in any way proved wrong. Based on this evidence, the judge ordered that the enforcement of Act 590 be permanently prohibited.

The decision was a blow from which creationists have never fully recovered. To make matters worse, a challenge to another law in Louisiana that favored equal time for creation, *Edwards v. Aguillard,* dragged on for five years.[18] Once again the creationists lost and the law was overturned. Efforts in federal courts fared no better.

## LOCAL EFFORTS

There were, however, other ways for the creationists to exert their influence. Many began developing a grassroots approach. This involved activism on the local level. More and more creationists entered and succeeded at local politics. They found positions on school boards and city councils. Creationist teachers went to court and sued, on the grounds that their individual rights were being hindered because they were forbidden to teach creationism.

By 1993, a First Amendment watchdog organization called People for the American Way reported that they had been monitoring about 500 political campaigns involving the Religious Right. Fundamentalist Christian candidates had won about 40 percent of those local elections.[19] Most of the campaigns had been organized by the Christian Coalition. Other Christian Right candidates had been helped by an organization called Citizens for Excellence in Education, whose purpose is to influence school curriculum. These candidates had a wide agenda that included outlawing abortion, monitoring school reading matter, and curbing sex education; but most of them also opposed the teaching of evolution without equal time for creationism.

That same year, in a San Diego suburb called Vista, Fundamentalists won a majority of seats on the school board. Although the new board failed to place creationism on the curriculum because of existing court rulings against it, they did pass a resolution requiring prayer at the start of their meetings. By 1995, the number of like-minded Fundamentalists on school boards had increased. It was estimated that they were a majority on more than 2,200 school boards around the country.[20]

Meanwhile, individual creationist teachers were looking for ways to assert their views. Like some creationist parents, they felt squelched and disregarded by their community's system of education. In 1991, a high school biology teacher in Orange County, California, named John Peloza filed a $5-million lawsuit against his school district, claiming that his constitutional rights had been violated because he had been forced to teach evolution.[21] The teacher had already been reprimanded by his district because he had been teaching his students that there was evidence for an "intelligent creator." According to the school district, as well as the state guidelines, evolution was to be taught as the only scientific theory that can explain the origin of life. The teacher claimed that he believed that creationism and evolutionism were merely different philosophies. According to him, the district was violating his freedom of speech as well as his academic freedom.

It took three years for the federal court to figure out how to treat the teacher's petition. Finally, it was decided not to give him permission to present his case against the school district. The case was thrown out, and the court never got to hear it. However, that same year, 1994, a college professor in favor of equal time for creationism won a similar battle in a different setting.[22] His name is Dean Kenyon, and he is the co-author of a controversial high school biology textbook called *Of Pandas and People*, which some school boards have tried to adopt. Although Kenyon does not consider himself a strict creationist, *Of Pandas and People* presents the idea that life's creation must have been guided by an "intelligent designer" and is indeed the product of the "intelligent shaping of matter." Kenyon had also defended creationist ideas for government officials in 1986 during the Louisiana battle, but that equal-time law had been later overturned by the Supreme Court.

At the time the controversy over him erupted, Kenyon had been teaching introductory biology at San Francisco State for more than ten years and had been presenting both evolutionist and creationist theories in his classroom. There had been complaints from some students and members of his department during that period, and in 1994, five students signed a letter claiming that Kenyon was giving very little coverage of evolutionary theory and too much coverage of creationist ideas. Kenyon countered by insisting that he was giving equal time to both theories. The complaint led to the biology department banning Kenyon from teaching the introductory biology course on the grounds that he was spreading propaganda in favor of religion. To the astonishment of many, the academic senate, composed of Kenyon's fellow teachers, disagreed. They charged that Kenyon's academic freedom had been violated by the ban. Then the American Association of University Professors rose to his defense, and his right to teach the course was reinstated.

Kenyon's case is unusual in that the majority of his supporters were neither fellow scientists nor professed believers in the creationist cause. They came from all disciplines, and some were more sensitive to the idea of academic freedom than they were to the issue of what constitutes true science. Hollis Matson, a health-education lecturer, may have summed up their attitude when she said, "I'm sitting here thinking about the things I say in my class, and if anyone else is sitting here doing the same thing, we're thinking about our own loss of academic freedom. I also think of what trouble I can get into when I talk about acupuncture as a healing science. It can't be proven in any laboratory."[83]

## RECENT STRATEGIES IN FAVOR OF EVOLUTION

It's true that, in recent years, there have been small gains on the part of some individual creationists and some creationist groups in the courts and in education. However, intellectual status has remained mostly in the evolutionist camp. Whereas the mainstream media finds good "copy" in the stories of creationist crusaders and their grassroots efforts in school districts and communities, they still implicitly favor the opinions of evolutionists and the mainstream scientific establishment. That is one reason why most supporters of evolution theory have not felt it necessary to take their credo to court or before academic senates.

Nevertheless, scientists and teachers in favor of evolution theory have been working to ensure the primacy of evolution education. In 1995, for example, the National Association of Biology Teachers published an official paper called "Statement on Teaching Evolution." In it, they made the strong assertion that evolution is an "unsupervised, impersonal, unpredictable natural process."[24] The phrase, in no uncertain terms, expressed their belief that the development of life on Earth cannot be understood in terms of "divine guidance" and that biology teaching must impart evolutionary ideas. Although noted religious historian Huston Smith and philosopher Alvin Plantinga wrote the association to complain that the assertion was too strong and more philosophical than scientific, the association decided to stick with it.

*Wesley Roberts, an ecology and biology teacher in Nashville, Tennessee, is poised to challenge state legislation threatening termination for any teacher who presents evolution as a fact in the classroom.*

In the last few years, biology scholars and researchers, who were perhaps unwilling or too busy to engage in court battles or public skirmishes with creationists, have been spreading the word about evolution and countering the ideas of creationists on the internet. A good example of such a phenomenon is the Talk.Origins Archive at http://www.talkorigins.org/. The archives were set up as a supplement to the Talk.Origins Usenet group, which is dedicated to discussing the evolution-creation controversy. Talk.Origins is a forum for both evolutionist and creationist users of the internet, but it is admittedly more favorable to the mainstream scientific point of view.

The Talk.Origins Archive is a comprehensive collection of scholarly and scientific articles on the debate, with a heavy emphasis on biology but including articles on catastrophism, theology, and geology. The archive's stated purpose is to "provide mainstream scientific responses to the many frequently asked questions (FAQs) and frequently rebutted assertions that appear in talk.origins." The FAQ file in Talk.Origins Archive is a patient explanation of the fundamental bases of current evolutionary thought in the question-and-answer form characteristic of most FAQ files. It takes into account the probable objections of creationists and answers them one by one. Following are a few examples from this file:

Q: I thought evolution was just a theory. Why do you call it a fact?

A: Biological evolution is a change in the genetic characteristics of a population over time. That this happens is a fact. Biological evolution also refers to the common descent of living organisms from shared ancestors. The evidence for historical evolution—genetic, fossil, anatomical, etc.—is so overwhelming that it is also considered a fact. The theory of evolution describes the mechanisms that cause evolution. So evolution is both a fact and a theory.

Q: Don't you have to be an atheist to accept evolution?

A: No. Many people of Christian and other faiths accept evolution as the scientific explanation for biodiversity.

Q: Isn't evolution just an unfalsifiable[25] tautology?

A: No. Evolutionary theory is in exactly the same condition as any other valid scientific theory, and many criticisms of it that rely on philosophy are misguided.

Q: If evolution is true, then why are there so many gaps in the fossil record? Shouldn't there be more transitional fossils?

A: Due to the rarity of preservation and the likelihood that speciation occurs in small populations during geologically short periods of time, transitions between species are uncommon in the fossil record. Transitions at higher taxonomic levels, however, are abundant.

The Talk.Origins Archive also offers an abundance of articles on theistic evolution, on some major misconceptions about evolution, and about the age of the Earth. Creationists would say that the site is biased, because many of the articles favor evolutionist explanations for life's origins. However, the material on the site is free of belligerence or defensiveness and is intended to open and ease the debate between the different points of view.

Meanwhile, a few individuals are putting great effort into finding a common ground on which people of all points of view can participate in discussing the origins of life on Earth. One of the most striking examples of an attempt to find that common ground is the work of retired physicist Thomas Gilbert. Gilbert left his job as a physicist at Argonne National Laboratory in 1987. In the eleven years that followed, he conceived and directed an enormous collaborative effort to present yearly lectures on life's origins. His project, known familiarly as "the Epic Project," is called "The Epic of Creation: Scientific, Biblical, and Theological Perspectives on Our Origins." Each year it brings together scientists, biblical scholars, and members of the clergy from around the world to the Lutheran School of Theology in Chicago. In 1998, the series began with lectures about the beginnings of life on Earth by ten scientists from a variety of fields. This was followed by stories of creation from the Old and New Testaments, which were then analyzed and interpreted by biblical scholars familiar with the historical background of the stories. The goal of the lecture series is to show that religion and science do not necessarily have to approach each other from a hostile perspective.

Perhaps Gilbert's lecture series will ease some of the tensions between evolutionists and creationists. Or perhaps, despite his efforts and the efforts of others, the argument will continue raging as fiercely as it has in the last sixty years or so. In many ways, the two extremes of the debate have moved much further apart then they were in 1858, when Darwin first announced his theory. In fact as scientific data from evolutionists accumulate, faith in creationism among its adherents only seems to grow stronger. What is more, there probably never will be an easy solution to a debate that pits more than a hundred years of tradition in scientific method against a centuries-old belief in the supernatural.

On the other hand, to look at the evolution-creation debate in terms too simple is a grave mistake. Between the scientific atheists who shun all notions of spirituality when it comes to explaining the workings of nature and the strict fundamentalists who insist on a literal interpretation of the Bible, there are many degrees. It's true that there are some "missing links" in the long continuum of opinions. But the only hope for peace among the two sides of the debate lies in a closer examination of the uncharted territory between them. Then perhaps, one day, the evolution-creation debate will cease to become a sensational topic exploited by the mainstream media. The focus of the debate may then move away from politics, the courts, and school boards into a more scholarly arena. Here it will finally resume its deserved place among the great intellectual debates of human history.

# The Debate in a Nutshell

The creation-evolution debate is a long continuum, with strict creationism at one extreme and pure Darwinism at the other. Between the two are a host of positions that rely more or less upon the Bible or upon mainstream scientific method. The basic disagreements between the two positions can be summed up fairly simply. In 1981, Act 590 of the Arkansas legislature set them forth in the following chart:

## THE CREATIONIST POSITION

1. The universe, energy, and life were created from nothing.

2. Mutation and natural selection could not by themselves have brought about the development of all living things from a single organism.

3. The originally created kinds of plants and animals may have changed, but only within fixed limits.

4. Man and apes have separate ancestries.

5. The Earth's geology can be explained by Catastrophism, including the occurrence of a worldwide flood.

6. The Earth and living kinds came into existence recently.

## The Evolutionist Position

1. Through naturalistic processes, the universe emerged from disordered matter and life emerged from nonlife.

2. Mutation and natural selection are sufficient to explain the development of present living kinds from simple earlier kinds.

3. Present living kinds emerged from simple earlier kinds by mutation and natural selection.

4. Man emerged from a common ancestor with apes.

5. The earth's geology and the evolutionary sequence can be explained by uniformitarianism.*

6. The earth came into existence several billion years ago and life came into existence somewhat later.

*Note:* Uniformitarianism is a doctrine stating that modern geological processes are sufficient to account for all geological changes in the past.

# Notes

1. "Town Divided over Whether to Teach Creationism." Special to the *New York Times* (February 13, 1995), p. A13.
2. Ronald L. Numbers, *The Creationists* (New York: Alfred A. Knopf, 1992), pp. 4–6.
3. Ibid.
4. Numbers, p. 4.
5. Numbers, p 7.
6. Numbers, pp. 13–18.

Chapter 2
1. Raymond A. Eve and Francis B. Harrold, *The Creationist Movement in Modern America.* Boston: Twayne Publishers, 1991, p. 17.
2. Eve and Harrold, pp. 3–4.
3. Richard N. Ostling, "Evangelicalism," *Microsoft Encarta,* CD-ROM, 1993.
4. Rev. Eugene Carlson Blake, "Fundamentalism," *Microsoft Encarta,* CD-ROM, 1993.
5. Eve and Harrold, pp. 40–44.
6. Eve and Harrold, pp. 3–4.
7. Numbers, pp. xii–xiii.
8. "Research Reveals News Agency's Role in Proceedings of Scopes Trial," *Smithsonian Research Reports,* Winter 1994.
9. Numbers, pp. 72–73.

10. Numbers, pp. 98–99.
11. Numbers, p. 73.
12. Eve and Harrold, pp. 26-27.
13. Ibid.


Chapter 3
  1. Numbers, p. 76.
  2. Numbers, p. 81.
  3. Numbers, p. 118.
  4. Numbers, p. 158.
  5. Madalyn Murray O'Hair, Address at Memphis State University, Memphis, Tennessee, Oct. 12, 1986. Transcript provided by American Atheist Press, Austin, Texas.
  6. Numbers, p. 202–203.
  7. Ibid.
  8. Ibid.
  9. Numbers, p. 80.
10. Numbers, pp. 203–204
11. Ibid.
12. Ibid.
13. "A Brief Statement of the History and Aims of the CRS," *Christian Research Society Quarterly* 19:149.
14. "A Decade of Creationist Research," Part I, *Creation Research Society Quarterly* (June 1975), 12(1): 3–36.
15. Numbers, p. 228
16. "History and Aims of the Creation Research Society," adapted and updated from W. H. Rusch, 1982, *Christian Research Society Quarterly* 19: 149.


Chapter 4
  1. Duane T. Gish, "A Decade of Creationist Research," Part II, *Creation Research Society Quarterly* (June 1975), (1):34–46.

2. Glen W. Wolform, "The 1993 Midwest Floods and Rapid Canyon Formation," *Creation Research Society Quarterly* (September 1994), 31(2): 109.
3. Gish, "A Decade of Creationist Research," Part I.
4. Ibid.
5. Ibid.
6. Ibid.
7. Gish, "A Decade of Creationist Research," Part II.
8. *Creation Matters,* a bimonthly publication of the Creation Research Society, Vol. 1, No. 4 (July/August 1996).
9. Gish, "A Decade of Creationist Research," Part II.


Chapter 5
1. Numbers, p. 45.
2. Carol Kaesuk Yoon, "Parallel Plots in Classic of Evolution," *New York Times* (November 12, 1996), p. C1.
3. Helder in *Creation Matters.*
4. John Horgan, "Stephen Jay Gould: Escaping in a Cloud of Ink," *Scientific American* 273(2): 37–41.
5. Stephen Jay Gould, "The Evolution of Life on the Earth," Part I, *Scientific American* 271(4): 84–91.
6. Frederic Golden, "A Kinder, Gentler Stephen Jay Gould," *Los Angeles Times* (October 8, 1996), p. E1.
7. Ibid.
8. Carol Kaesuk Yoon, "Biologists Recreate the Birth of a Flower Species: How Much of a Role Does Chance Play in Determining History?" *New York Times* (May 7, 1996), Science Times Section.
9. Ibid.
10. Ibid.
11. Eve and Harrold, p. 77.
12. Eve and Harrold, p. 75.
13. Eve and Harrold, p.73.
14. John Nobel Wilford, "2.3-Million-Year-Old Jaw

Extends Human Family, *New York Times* (November 19, 1996), Science Times Section.

15. John Noble Wilford, "The Transforming Leap, from 4 legs to 2," in *New York Times* (September 5, 1995), Science Times Section.
16. Numbers, p. 240.

Chapter 6

1. Eve and Harrold, pp. 94–96.
2. J. Moffet, *Storm in the Mountains* (Carbondale, Ill.: Southern Illinois University Press), p. 14. Quoted in Eve and Harrold, p. 97.
3. Eve and Harrold, pp.94–96.
4. Ibid.
5. "Public Acceptance of Human Evolution," from "The Scientifically Illiterate," *American Demographics* 9(6): 26–31.
6. Stephen R. S. Clark, "In the Beginning Was What?" *New York Times* (January 10, 1993), Section 7, CD-ROM version.
7. Eve and Harrold, p. 104.
8. Robert Sullivan, "An Army of the Faithful," *New York Times* (April 25, 1993), Sect. 6, CD-ROM version.
9. Ibid.
10. Numbers, pp. 146–147.
11. Numbers, pp. 147–149.
12. Ibid.
13. *McLean v. Arkansas Board of Education*, 529 F. Supp. 1255 (E.D. Ark. 1982)
14. Eve and Harrrold, p. 149
15. Ibid.
16. Eve and Harrold, p. 150
17. *Everson v. Board of Education*, 330 U.S. 1, 15-16 (1947), quoted in *McLean V. Arkansas Board of Education*.

18. *Edwards v. Aguillard* 482 U.S. 578 (1987); *Aguillard v. Treen,* No. 81-4787, slip op., (E.D. La. Jan. 10, 1985).

19. Seth Mydans, "Political Proving Ground for the Christian," *New York Times* (February 20, 1993), Sec. 1, CD-ROM version.

20. Goodman, Walter. "Exploring the Crusade of Anti-Darwinians," *New York Times* (May 30, 1995), Section C, CD-ROM version.

21. "Suit over Evolution Created: Rights Violated, Says State Biology Teacher," *San Jose Mercury News* Oct. 1, 1991.

22. Laura Kurtzman, Teacher Wins Fight Over Creationism," *San Jose Mercury News* January 11, 1994, p. 1A.

23. Ibid.

24. Quoted in Steve Kloehn, "On Second Thought, Biology Teachers Leave Room for God," *Chicago Tribune* (October, 17, 1997), online version.

25. Scientists believe that genuine scientific hypotheses are falsifiable, meaning that they have the potential of being proved false by other arguments and fresh data. An unfalsifiable tautology is a circular statement that can never be proved wrong, such as the statement, "The sky is blue because it is blue."

# For Further Reading

Dawkins, Richard. 1986. *The Blind Watchmaker: Why the Evidence of Evolution Reveals a Universe Without Design.* New York: W. W. Norton. The author takes an in-depth look at natural selection and shows how to his mind it effectively counters any claims of development guided by an intelligent designer.

Dennet, Daniel C. 1995. *Darwin's Dangerous Idea: Evolution and the Meanings of Life.* New York: Simon and Schuster. A far-reaching examination of the repercussions of Darwin's views. The author examines how Darwinism destroys the notion that the human species is at the center of the universe as well as most supernatural beliefs.

Denton, Michael. 1986. *Evolution: A Theory in Crisis.* Bethesda, Md.: Adler and Adler. A scientific critique of evolution, mostly from the standpoint of molecular biology, by a man who is not a typical creationist but feels there are too many gaps in Darwinian evolution to overlook.

Eldredge, Niles. 1995. *Reinventing Darwin: The Great Debate at the High Table of Evolutionary Theory.* New York: John Wiley & Sons. The co-author of the famous article "Punctuated Equilibria" (with Stephen Jay Gould) introduces us to a debate within the evolution camp: ultra-Darwinians and the Eldredge-Gould "naturalists."

Eve, Raymond A., and Francis B. Harrold. 1991. *The Creationist Movement in Modern America.* Boston: Twayne Publishers. A patient and well-researched survey of creationism as a social, historical, political, and religious movement.

Frye, Roland M., ed. 1983. *Is God a Creationist? The Religious Case Against Creation-Science.* New York: Scribner's. Eleven articles by authors of differing theological backgrounds, all of whom object to creationism.

Gish, Duane. *Evolution: The Challenge of the Fossil Record.* San Diego, Calif.: Creation-Life Publishers, 1985. A point-by-point attack on conventional interpretations of the fossil record by one of the most outspoken proponents of scientific creationism.

Gould, Stephen J. 1977. *Ever Since Darwin: Reflections in Natural History.* New York: W. W. Norton. Gould's strong positions on science, evolution, skepticism, and the scientific method are explained for the layperson.

Kitcher, Philip. 1982. *Abusing Science: The Case Against Creationism.* Cambridge, Mass.: MIT Press. An attack on creationism from the point of view of the history and philosophy of science.

La Follette, Marcel C., ed. 1983. *Creationism, Science, and the Law: The Arkansas Case.* Cambridge, Mass.: The MIT Press. The volume presents the full text of the Arkansas Creation Science Law 590, as well as excerpts from legal briefs from both sides and 14 articles about various aspects of the trial.

McGowan, Chris. 1984. *In the Beginning: A Scientist Shows Why the Creationists Are Wrong.* New York: Prometheus Books. Written by a well-known paleontologist, this book offers evidence for evolution mostly through a discussion of the fossil record.

Morris, Henry M., ed. 1985. *Scientific Creationism.* Revised edition. San Diego, Calif.: Creation-Life. The definitive book of the creationist position, edited by one of the founders of creation science.

Numbers, Ronald L. 1992. *The Creationists.* New York: Alfred A. Knopf. The most complete history of the creationist movement. Written by a historian of science and medicine who was raised in a Seventh-Day Adventist family of ministers. He is no longer a creationist, but in writing this book was "committed to treating its advocates with the same respect I might accord evolutionists."

Sagan, Carl. 1996. *The Demon-Haunted World: Science as a Candle in the Dark.* New York: Random House. Sagan's attack on what he considers pseudoscience and superstition and his hymn to what he considers the wondrous realm of true science.

Weiner, Jonathan. 1994. *The Beak of the Finch.* New York: Alfred A. Knopf, 1994. A book documenting the work of biologists Peter and Rosemary Grant, who studied many generations of finches on a Galapagos island for more than 20 years. The Grants claim that because evolution takes place so quickly on the small island as a result of abrupt environmental changes, they were able to document and finally calculate the process of survival of the fittest.

Youngblood, Ronald J. 1991. *The Book of Genesis: An Introductory Commentary.* Grand Rapids, Mich.: Baker Book House. Written by a member of the team that produced the New International Version of the Bible, favored by Fundamentalists. However, the author believes in an ancient Earth and a local flood.

# Index